D1860214

A
MUNDARI ENGLISH DICTIONARY

A
MUNDARI ENGLISH DICTIONARY

MANINDRA BHUSAN BHADURI

GYAN

Published by

Gyan Publishing House
5, Ansari Road
Daryaganj, New Delhi-110002
Phone: 011-47034999, 9811692060
E-mail: books@gyanbooks.com

Distribution Network
gyanbooks.com
India, USA, Canada, UK, Australia, France

© Publisher

All rights reserved. No part of this work may be reproduced, stored, adapted, or transmitted in any form or by any means, electronic, mechanical, photocopying, micro-filming, recording or otherwise, or translated in any language, without the prior written permission of the copyright owner and the publisher.

ISBN : 978-81-212-4465-7 (PB)
First Published, Calcutta, 1931

2nd Impression 2020

Printed at: Gyan Press, Delhi.

The book is sold subject to the condition that it shall not, by way of trade or otherwise, be lent, resold, hired out, or otherwise circulated without the prior publisher's written consent.

The book at your disposal is the edition of an old book originally published long back. The Text quality of this book may not be at par as compared to our other books but many readers approached us to reprint this important book so that it could satiate their hunger. We request all the readers of this book to help us to improve its quality by providing the necessary text of those pages which are not properly visible. Your valuable support in this case will be highly appreciated and acknowledged and our future readers will be benefitted immensely.

To

The Memory

of

My Revered Father

The Late Prof. SASI BHUSAN BHADURI

INTRODUCTORY NOTE

I feel some diffidence in writing a foreword to this book for although I do not claim any credit or accept any responsibility for the book, as it now stands, it came to be compiled at my suggestion and it has developed out of a small vocabulary collected by me over twenty years ago while I was learning the language. As my manuscript used to be borrowed now and again by friends in the judicial and executive services of Government who wanted to pass their language examination, I thought that a more comprehensive vocabulary might be of greater practical value. As the author of the present volume ordinarily resides in the heart of the Munda country and knows the language and is interested in such studies I suggested to him the usefulness of such a compilation if he could spare the time and labour necessary to prepare it. He readily welcomed the idea and I lent him my manuscript and discussed with him the proper method of enlarging the vocabulary and making it more accurate and helpful to general students, and, to some extent, to scientific students as well. I am glad to find that in the three years that has since elapsed the author has with characteristic energy and industry availed himself of his opportunities and enlarged the vocabulary. In some instances, though unfortunately not in all, he has indicated the source from which a word appears to have been borrowed by the Mundas and in some others he has noted allied words in some cognate language or other. The reader should not forget that in some cases the English equivalent of a Mundari term is necessarily imperfect, as connoting either too much or too little, for the categories of primitive people are often different from those of the civilised. But such imperfections are inevitable in a book which does not aspire to be more than a mere glossary of words for the use of the beginner in the study of the language for practical purposes. I congratulate the author on this useful compilation made by him in the intervals of his professional work as a lawyer. The book, I trust, will be found useful by those for whom it is intended.

RANCHI,
The 17th September, 1929.

SARAT CHANDRA ROY

PREFACE

The Mundari language is spoken by the Mundas and the allied tribes living in the Chota Nagpur plateau and in parts of Assam where a large number of Mundas have emigrated as tea garden labourers. The dialects of the Mundari family of speech, to which Santali, Birhor and other tongues belong, are besides Chota Nagpur, also spoken in the Santal Perganas which adjoin some of the Bengal districts and in some of what are called the Garhjat states, to the south of Chota Nagpur.*

This geographical distribution of the Mundari family of speech is one of the causes of the presence of a large number of Indo-Aryan words in the Munda and Santal vocabularies. On the other hand, there are a number of words surprisingly common to Mundari, Hindi and Bengali which have no Sanskrit roots, *e.g.*, *Bānāi* (noun form of Bāi, to make, to prepare, to build, to create)—making, creation, in Mundari, *Bānāoṭi* in the same sense in Hindi and *Bānāna* in the same sense in Bengali; *Ḍumbui*, to sink (Munda), *Ḍubānā* (Hindi), *Ḍubāna* (Bengali). In such cases, it is difficult to say who were the borrowers.

For the purpose of comparison Sanskrit, Bengali, Hindi, Santali and Birhor dialects have been chosen, necessarily in view of my own limitations for which

* The number of Munda-speaking people is estimated at 624,506 by the census of 1921.

I have to apologise. It has not been possible for me to point out all the analogous words in those dialects. The Santali and Birhor words have been given in many cases, though not in all, to show the nature of the changes that have occurred in those dialects.

The compilation of this book was in a way accidental. About 5 years ago I happened to come across a small exercise book containing *a list of about 600 words* belonging to my esteemed friend Rai Bahadur S. C. Roy, M.A., B.L., M.L.C., of Ranchi. I asked him if he could devote a little time and make it into a really useful book of Mundari vocabulary for which there had been a long-felt want. He replied that he had very little time, threw the whole burden upon me and asked me to undertake the work which I did, not without hesitation. I do not know how far I have been successful in discharging that burden, but I am fully conscious that the book cannot claim to contain a full and complete list of all Mundari words and their variants as spoken in different parts of the country. This means a stupendous work which is impossible for one who has to devote most of his time to his own profession. I shall however consider my labours amply repaid if the book proves useful to those who want to learn the language.

Besides my debt to the Rai Bahadur which I gratefully acknowledge I am grateful to late Babu Santosh Bodra for the valuable assistance he had been giving me in the compilation of this book till he was cut off by the cruel hand of death in the midst of the work.

I also owe a debt to my friends Mr. H. J. B. le Patourel, late S. D. O. of Khunti, who helped me by the loan of his copy of the *Santali Dictionary* and

Mr. Nabendu Bhusan Mukherjee and Babu Suleman Purti who kindly went through the proof-sheets.

I owe to my nephew Dr. Prabodh Chandra Bagchi, M.A., Dr. ès Lettres (Paris), the publication of this book by the Calcutta University and the correction of several of the proof-sheets. Lastly I have to express my thanks to the University Press for the trouble they have taken in the printing of the book.

The book in its present form was completed and handed over to the Calcutta University in the beginning of 1928. New words have since been included in an Addendum.

KHUNTI (RANCHI),
December, 1929.

M. BHADURI

NOTE ON PRONUNCIATION

The diacritic marks adopted in this book are generally those followed in the J. B. O. R. S. for Sanskrit scripts.

Vowels.

a corresponds to the Sanskrit अ and is pronounced like *a* in 'call.'

ā	,,	,,	आ	,,	,,	*a* in 'father.'
i	,,	,,	इ	,,	,,	*i* in 'pit.'
ī	,,	,,	ई	,,	,,	*ee* in 'heed.'
u	,,	,,	उ	,,	,,	*u* in 'put.'
ū	,,	,,	ऊ	,,	,,	*oo* in 'pool.'
e	,,	,,	ए	,,	,,	*e* in 'pet.'
o	,,	,,	ओ	,,	,,	*o* in 'pole.'

When two vowels stand side by side, they retain their original sounds; they do not coalesce and make a midsound. When vowels are nasalised, *n* in italics is placed after the vowels.

Consonants.

The consonants *f*, *q*, *v*, *x*, *z* do not exist.

b corresponds to the Sanskrit ब *b* in 'box.'

bh ,, ,, भ

c is never used like *c* in 'circle.'

ch corresponds to the Sanskrit च and is pronounced like *ch* in 'chicken.'

chh corresponds to the Sanskrit

d	,,	,,	द	as	*th* in 'thy.'
ḍ	,,	,,	ड	,,	*d* in 'door.'
dh	,,	,,	ध		
ḍh	,,	,,	ढ	,,	*dh* in "dhow.'
g	,,	,,	ग	,,	*g* in 'get.'
h	,,	,,	ह	,,	*h* in 'horse.'
gh	,,	,,	घ		
j	,,	,,	ज	,,	midway between *dg* in 'hedge' and *j* in 'justice.'
k	,,	,,	क	,,	*k* in 'kill.'
kh	,,	,,	ख		
l	,,	,,	ल	,,	*l* in 'lame.'
m	,,	,,	म	,,	*m* in 'man.'
p	,,	,,	प	,,	*p* in 'pen.'
ph	,,	,,	फ	,,	*ph* in 'philosophy.'
r	,,	,,	र	,,	*r* in 'door.'
ṛ	,,	,,	ड़	,,	second *r* in 'reward.'
s	,,	,,	स	,,	*s* in 'sun.'
sh	,,	,,	ष	,,	*sh* in 'shun.'
t	,,	,,	त	,,	*th* in 'plinth' without the aspirate *h*.
th	,,	,,	थ	,,	*th* in 'throw.'
ṭ	,,	,,	ट	,,	*t* in 'tree.'
ṭh	,,	,,	ठ		
n	,,	,,	न;		

when it occurs in the beginning of a word, it is pronounced like the *n* in 'no'; when it occurs before *g*, it is pronounced like the Sanskrit ङ, or as in the English word 'sing;' but when *ng* is followed by another vowel, it is pronounced like *ng* in 'finger' the *g* sound being distinct, never like 'danger.' When *n* occurs before *k* it is pronounced like *nk* in 'sink;' but when the *n* belongs to the prefixes *en* or *in* the *n* sound is to be distinctly pronounced.

The sign (′) represents the peculiarly checked sounds of vowels and the consonants 'b' and 'd,' *e.g.*, the checked consonants in **āb′**, ub′, **ānjed′**, **med′** and the checked vowels in **ārā′**, bā′, be′, de′. In both the consonants and the vowels, the sound is at first checked and then released slowly ; thus in the case of vowels, it seems to have the sound of two vowels, one distinct and short, and the other indistinct and long drawn out ; and in the case of the consonant *b*— the first distinct sound of 'b' seems to be followed by the sound of an indistinct '*m*,' and in the case of the consonant '*d*,' the first distinct sound of '*d*' seems to be followed by the sound of an indistinct '*n*.'

A

MUNDARI-ENGLISH DICTIONARY

A

Ā—(1) present indeterminate tense suffix, signifying 'is or 'is in the habit of': *e.g.*, Ne jo sibilā—This fruit is sweet; Hoṛoko jānāge ko jojomā—Mundas eat anything;
(2) possessive suffix;
(3) emphatic personal pronoun prefix: *e.g.*, in āling, ām, āpe;
(4) intransitive future tense suffix: *e.g.*, bāioā—will do;
(5) a prefix meaning 'absence of' or 'without';
(6) simple future suffix.

Āā—bow.

Āā-sar—bow and arrow.

Āb'—to wash the face.

Ābā / **Ābā-gā** —father: commonly used in the vocative case by children.

Ābar—weak (H. Nābar).

Ābasthā—condition: Syn. Dasā, Hālat (H.).

Āben—you (dual): also used as a singular indicating respect.

Āben-ā—your (dual).

Ābe-Tābe—about to; on the point of.

Ābgā—nice; pure (sometimes used contemptuously).

Abhāgā—unlucky (H.).

Ablā—feeble; helpless (H.).

Abodh—ignorant (H.).

Ābrum—to hatch (S. Obor).

Ābu—we (including the person speaking and the person addresed, *i.e.*, you and I).

Ābuā—our (dual).

Ābung—to wash the hands and feet.

Achākā—unexpectedly ; suddenly (H.).

Āchāṛā—to sow paddy in mud : Syn. Lewa.

Āchrāel bongā—protecting spirit.

Āchu—to order ; to employ in service ; to command ; to ask.

Āchu'—to sneeze (Beng. Hānchi).

Āchuni—one who commands.

Āchuini—one who is commanded ; a servant.

Āchur—to reach ; to arrive ; to rise.

Ād'—to lose ; to miss.

Āḍ'- / Oṛo, hāḍo }—and (H. Āur ; Beng. Āro).

Ādākānā—lost ; a thing lost.

Ādbud—enormous.

Āder—to take inside ; to enter inside ; to go in (H. Andar).

Adharmi—unjust ; unrighteous (H.).

Ādi—ginger (H.).

Āding—inner apartment of a house set apart for worship, preferably kitchen.

Āḍoā-chāuli—rice husked without being boiled.

Ādol-hukum—to disregard or disobey an order.

Āḍṛā āḍṛi—to face each other preparatory to fight.

Ādrak—ginger (H.).

Ādwāti—enmity (H.).

Āe—it ; he.

Āeā—its ; his.

Āe-ā-gā—his ; its.

Āe-ār—front ; preceding ; before ; previous ; first ; to precede ; to conduct ; to lead (Sant. Ayur).

Āe-ār hisā—fore part.

Āeār-kāji—prophecy : Syn. [illegible]-Kān-Kāji.

Āeār Kājini—prophet ; seer.

Āeār-o—to go in front ; to go ahead ; to advance.

Āeār-re—in front of ; before ; previously.

Āeār-te—ahead ; in front.

Āe-ge—he himself (reflexive).

Āe-ke—to him.

Āe-te—by itself.

Āgam—to foreknow (H.).

Āgar—if (H.).

Āgardigar—forward and backward.

Aghān—the month of Aghān (H.).

Āghrāo—to refuse obstinately.

Āgotar—in advance.

Āgrāo—to wait for a better bargain (said of intending vendors).

Āguadār—leader ; those who precede a marriage party ; negotiator of a marriage.

Āgu }
Āu } —to bring.

Āguākān—*adj.*, applies to the thing brought.

Āguni—one who brings.

Āh'—alas.

Āhrā—narrow lowland (Don), through which water flows.

Āh'-re }
Āh'-uh' } —an expression of dissappointment and regret.

Āil—to jump.

Āin—law.

Āing, Ing—I.

Āingā—my ; mine.

Āing Kā-ge—*lit.*, not I, *i.e.*, I am not the man.

Āiṭhāo—to twist lightly ; to squeeze (H.).

Āium—to hear.

Āium-Kumṛu—to listen stealthily ; to overhear ; to spy.

Ājā—grand-father or grand-uncle : Syn. Tāṭā. (H.).

Ajāit—to outcaste (S. Ojat).

Ajas—to blame; to accuse (Sant. Ardas : *cf.* Apajaś—infamy; disrepute—Beng. and H.).

Ājāuri—to empty; leisure (H.).

Ājbājāo—to entangle.

Ajgar—powerful; vast (H.).

Āji—grand-mother or grand-aunt; elder sister.

Āji-hānār—wife's elder sister.

Āji-ledrā—the cloth given to the grand-mother of the bride.

Ājinātiā—relationship between grand-mother and grand-child.

Ājmāo—to examine (H.).

Ājom—to feed.

Ākā—an exclamation of pain.

Ākābākā—to be surprised; to be confused; to be taken aback; to wonder.

Ākādā—transitive past tense suffix.

Ākādāndā—to marvel; to wonder.

Ākāl—famine; scarcity : Syn. Janji (H., Sant. Ṭonṭā).

Akal-pakal—uneasy; restless.

Ākānā—intransitive past tense suffix.

A-kath—unspeakable (H.).

Ākbākāo, Ākbāki—to get confused; to gasp for want of breath (Sant. Ukbukāo).

Ākhāṛā—a place for dancing, or meeting in a village (Sant.).

Ākhir—end; last : Syn. Tāiom-utar, Ṭunḍu (H.).

Ākhring, Ākiring—to sell.

Ākid'—to put in; to take up; to take to a different place.

Ākil—sense.

Āking—those two; they (dual); both; the two.

Āklāhā.—sensible; wise.

Āko—they (plural).

Ākoā—their (plural).

Āko-ke—to them.

Āktear—power; control; authority; jurisdiction (Sant., H.).

Ālāng—we two (including addressee), *i.e.*, you and I.

Ālāngā—their and my.

Ālāng—tongue.

Ālāng—to sharpen ploughshares and other instruments by beating while red hot (H. Pājāo).

Ālchi—to prickle; to goad.

Āle—we (more than two), *i.e.*, they and I.

Āleā—our (more than two), *i.e.*, their and mine.

Ālgāo—to lift up (H.).

Āli—we (excluding the addressee).

Āli—to get damp and moist; moisture (Sant. Olahet').

Āling—we two (excluding addressee), *i.e.*, he and I.

Ālingā—his and my.

Ālo—prohibitive particle signifying 'do not,' 'don't.'

Āloben—don't you (two).

Ālokāko—don't they; let them not; (that) they may not.

Ālom—don't you (singular).

Ālope—don't you (more than two).

Ālpung—wave.

Ālsāngā—a kind of paddy.

Ālu—potato.

Ālu'—to strain out water by the hand.

Ām—you (singular).

Āmā—your (singular).

Amal—acidity (H.).

Āmdāni—income (H.).

Āmānat—to deposit : Syn. Do (H.).

Āmgā—used when addressing females; to draw attention.

Āmin } —to cleanse; to clear.
Āming }

Āmin—a surveyor.

Āminãng-ge—that much ; so much.

Ām-ke—to you.

Āmlā—officer of a court (H).

Ām-saphri—guava.

Āmṭhā—mango juice dried up into a paste.

Ānāchu }
Ānchu } —order ; command.

Anāchu—the act of sneezing.

Ānāguṛ—to get down ; to descend : Syn. Āṛgun.

Ānāj—grain (H.).

Anal-onol—habit of writing.

Ānāming—the act of clearing ; clearance.

Ānāpir—the act of flying.

Ānāṛi—newcomer ; inexperienced (H.).

Ānāṛid′—the act of looking or gazing ; gaze.

Anāsādi—satiety.

Ānāsi—prayer ; petition ; the act of asking.

Ānāsul—maintenance ; support ; the act of bringing up.

Ānāting—the act of grazing.

Ānāṛil—hailstone.

Ā*n*ch—heat, flame (H.).

Ā*n*chal—border of a cloth : Syn. Āchārā.

Ānchu—order; command ; rule ; law ; commandment.

Ānchu-itu—lawyer.

Āndā-ā—to fry (with oil) vegetables (Sant. Andak′) : Syn. Honḍā.

Āndāj—approximate ; by guess (H.).

Āndā-Tāwā—in hot haste.

Ānder-Ondoṛ—to walk aimlessly.

Āndhā—blind (H.).

Āndhā-Dhund—very greatly, severely (Sant., H.).

An-Dhan—wealth : Syn. Bābā chāuli.

Āndher—unjust; unlawful (Sant., H.).
Āndhi—blind (female): Syn. Poṛo (H.).
Andkul—very loud (Sant.).
Andhkup—great darkness (H.).
Āṅḍiā—male of animals, birds, etc., especially uncastrated bullocks; licentious; libidinous (Sant., H., Beng.).
Āndkā—untimely.
Andoṛ—to tease.
Andṛ-pandṛ—to step or speak irregularly, as when drunk.
Āndu—leg ornament; anklet.
Anduṛ-nanduṛ—hither and thither (Sant. Androk-sandrok).
Aneāe—unjust; injustice (Sant., H.).
Āng—to dawn.
Āngā—dress; coat (Sant.).
Āngāo—to wish; to desire (Sant.).
Āngidpāngid'—at the point of death (Sant. Angap angap).
Āngir—adultery (Sant.).
Āng'jānā—it is dawn.
Āngodipli—time of sunrise.
Āngore—at dawn.
Āngo-ipil—morning star; Venus.
Āngo-mā—daily; always. Āngo-mutid'—day by day; daily
An-hos—unconscious (Sant.).
An-hut—many.
Anjān—ignorant (H.).
Anjānti—by mistake (H.).
Ānjed'—to dry up; subside; to condense by boiling.
Anjli—a measure of things contained in the palm of the hands joined together.
Ankaṛi—hook; pitchfork.
An-kathā—Unspeakable (used in a good sense).

Ānkur }
Ānkuāo } —to germinate (H.): *cf.* Skt. Aṅkura.

Ānman—exactly.

Ān-pach—indigestion (H.).

Ān-pāni—food and drink: Syn. Jomeā-nuiā (H.).

Ānṛi—a kind of fig ripening in August (Sant. Ānjir).

Ānsā—to be satiated; to get tired (H., Beng.).

Ansbans—descendants (Sant., H.).

Ānt'—end; clue.

Āntar—measure of the distance between one furrow and another, made while ploughing the field.

Ānṭil—a punch used to make holes in iron.

Ānu—to overlay with any metal.

Ānu—to cause to drink; to suckle (Sant.).

Ānumān—to guess (Sans.).

Āoāj—sound; noise: Syn. Sāṛi (H.).

Āosān—to make easy; to lighten; leisure: Syn. Ajāuri (Sant., H. Ashān).

Āosār—chance; opportunity; leisure (H., Sant. Aphsor; Beng. Avasar).

Ā-pach—indigestion (H.).

Āpāchu—to command each other: reciprocal form of **Āchu.**

Āpāngiṛ—to have illicit connection; elopement.

Āpāṛid'—to see each other: reciprocal form of Ārid.

Āpe—more than two (H. Aplog; Beng. Apanārā).

Āpeā—you (more than two).

Āpe-ke—to you all.

Āphat—calamity; distress (Sant. Āphoti; H.).

Āphim—opium (H.).

Āpiā—the numeral three.

Āpil—appeal.

Āpi-mā—three days.

Āpir—to fly.

Āpnāo—to own; to make one's own; to occupy (H.).

Āpṛā—to part with.

Aprel—the month of April.

Āpṛānāsingi } —ploughing time; 7 A.M.
Āṛānāsingi }

Āprob—wings.

Āpsoch—regret (H., Beng. Āpsos).

Āpsul—to maintain each other: reciprocal form of Āsul.

Āpu—father (Sant., Beng. Bāp).

Āpuing—my father.

Āpu-ko—forefathers.

Āpuko-ete-nāmākān-te ā—ancestral.

Āpum—your father.

Āpum-ā—of your father.

Āpus—relation (H.).

Āputāko—their father.

Āputāle—our father.

Āpu-te—his father.

Ār—and; also; other: Syn. Oṛo; Haḍo (Sant.).

Āṛ-ā—edible leaves; vegetable (Sant. Aṛak).

Āṛā—to give up; to set free; to let loose (Sant. Aṛak': *cf.* Beng. Eṛā).

Ārā'—red (Sant. Arak: *cf.* Sans. Alaktaka).

Ārā—son-in-law; brother-in-law: used as a suffix to denote acquired relationship, *e.g.*, Hon-ārā, Misi-ārā.

Ārā'-hasa—red sandy earth.

Ārā-hon } —son-in-law.
Ārā-ing }

Āraj—prayer; petition (H.).

Āṛānā } —yoke of the plough (Sant. Ārar).
Ārā*nṛn*ā }

Ārānā-ipil } —the yoke constellation; Orion.
Har-juāiṭ }

Āṛāndi—marriage.

Āṛāndi-jopor }—a person of marriageable age, *i.e.*, a youth
Āṛāndi-jukur } of 15 or 16 or a girl of 13 or 14.

Āṛāndi-lijā—the cloth given by the bridegroom to the bride.

Āra*n*t—a warrant.

Āṛāo—to be disobedient; lazy; obstinate (Sant. Aḍṛao).

Ārasul—bloody dysentery (Sant. Araksul).

Ārath—meaning (Sansk. Artha; H.).

Āṛā-uṛu }—to hesitate; doubt; waver.
Āṛhā-uṛhu }

Ārdā—time; span of life.

Ardhāngi—Hemiplegia; paralysis.

Āreā—the numeral nine (Sant. Are).

Ārej′—to sprinkle water; to bale out water (Sant. Arech′).

Āṛgom }—harrow (Sant. to level).
Ātaṛgom }

Āṛgu }—to bring down; to come down.
Āṛgun }

Āri—to bellow (used of buffaloes only).

Āṛi—side; edge; border; ridge of a rice field: Syn. Chimi (Sant. Are).

Āṛid′—to gaze; to look at; to open the eyes (Sant. Arit′).

Āṛid′-rakab—to look up; to look upwards.

Āṛid-tārid′—to browbeat; to frown.

Āṛil—to hail; hailstone.

Ārkhā }—to covet; to wish for what another has got
Irkhā } (Sant.: *cf.* Sansk. Īrshā).

Ārkhi—beer distilled from Mohua.

Ārkid′—to run away with something; to carry off.

Arjaniā—one who earns (Sant., H.).

Arjāo—to earn; to raise crop (Sant.).

Ārjhā-ārjhi—to entangle: Syn. Hāṛā pāṭā (Sant.).

Ārjhāo—to entangle.

Ārji—to pray; to request; petition (Sant., H.).

Āṛkāṭhiā }
Āṛākāṭi } —a cooli recruiter (H.).

Āṛkāṭha—roof beam.

Āṛna—a buffalo of mature age.

Āṛoā—grain, sundried and husked.

Aṛosi-paṛosi—neighbourhood.

Arpā—sheaf of paddy (Sant.).

Arsal—to light up in order to see (Sant.).

Ārsāpiṭhā—a kind of cake.

Ārsi—mirror : Syn. Nel-umbul, Darpan, Parkalā (H.).

Ārtāng—to develop before ripening (fruits, etc.) : Syn. Gadar (H. Gadrānā).

Ārtāngsingi—just before sunrise, when the sky is red.

Ārti—hearse.

Āru-sāngā—a kind of edible root (H. Āru).

Aruch—dislike for food (H.).

Ās—turn ; time ; chance.

Āsādi—to satiate ; to be wearied or tired (H. Ānsā).

Asāi—eggs of flies (Sant. Asāe).

Āsāhādusāhā—bad ; despicable ; ill-omened (Sant.).

Āsal—principal ; chief ; pure ; true (H.).

Āsāmbher—uncontrollable ; that which cannot be checked or prevented.

Āsāmi—tenant ; opposite party in a suit ; debtor (Sant., H.).

Āsān usun—to awake from sleep and stir (Sant.).

Āsāṛh—the month of Āsārh (June-July) (Sant., H.).

Āsarphi—gold coin (Sant., H.).

Āsathi—false ; unfair (Sant., Sansk. Asat) : Syn. Hosoṛ.

Asat-osot—lazy ; unwilling (Sant.).

Ās-bharosā—hope (Sant., H.).

Āsepāse—near about ; close to (Sant.).

Āsi—to ask for ; to want ; to pray for something.

Āsin—the month of Āsin (September-October) (Sant., H.).

Āsirbād—blessings (Sant., H., Beng.).

Āskal—bird (Sant.).

Āskati—lazy ; dull ; tired ; to be tired (Sant.).

Āsnān—bath ; baptismal bath ; to baptise.

Āsra—to hope ; to expect help (H.).

Āsrae—refuge ; shelter (Sant., H.).

Āstābol—stable.

Āstin—sleeve (Sant., H.).

Āstir—patient ; calm (Sans. Sthir).

Asu } —very much.
Isu }

Āsul—to maintain ; to nourish ; to tame ; to bring up ; support ; cherish (Sant.).

Asur—greedy ; voracious.

Asur—the tribe that preceded the Mundas in Chota-Nagpur. According to legends, they were the first inhabitants of the earth and were iron smelters, whom the Sing Bonga destroyed on account of their iniquities, and changed their womenfolk into nature spirits.

Ās-us—to grumble ; to murmur.

Āṭā—flour ; gum (Sant., H.).

Ātā—to roast grain over fire ; to parch ; to fry (Sant.).

Āṭā—ambush (Sant.).

Āṭā-āṭi—to quarrel ; to dispute ; to argue (*cf.* Sant. Āḍrā āḍri).

Aṭal—row ; fold ; layer (Sant.).

Ātal-bā—a kind of flower.

Āṭal puṛu—a cup made of leaves doubled up (Sant. Atal puruk).

Atāng—to receive on the palm ; to spread out something.

Ataṛ—to burn ; to set fire to.

Ātāṛāgom—see Aṛgom.
Aṭā-sāṭa—close together.
Āte—with ; by means of (Beng., H.).
Āṭed'—to spread a bed : Syn. Bil (Sant. Atet'—to spread out).
Āṭghāṭ—opportunity ; secrets (Sant.).
Athā-h—bottomless ; very deep (Sant.).
Āthāuṛi—unknowingly (H.).
Āthāuṛi pāthāuṛi—aimlessly.
Aṭhwārā—*lit.* eight days ; a week.
Āṭi—bundle ; sheaf (Sant.).
Āṭikuṭi—various kinds : Syn. Ana-mana.
Āting—to graze (Sant. Atin).
Ātingir—to entice away : also used in a good sense, *e.g.*, to take away.
Āṭkāo—to prevent ; to stop (Sant.).
Āṭkār—to think ; to understand ; to know ; to feel ; to believe ; to consider ; to perceive (Sant.).
Āṭkir—a kind of creeper.
Atmā—spirit (H.).
Àtom—to remove ; to separate ; to go to one side ; side ; border ; edge ; brink.
Aṭpaṭāo—to struggle ; to be restless (Sant.).
Ātṛgom—see Aṛgom.
Ātu—to float ; to flow ; to be carried away by flood (Sant.).
Ātur—to winnow.
Āu—to bring : *cf.* Āgu-an—expression of surprise or regret.
Aual—first ; pure ; best (Sant., H.).
Āung-āung—growling of a tiger.
Āu*n* rāo—to get sour and stale.
Āurā—a kind of fruit (Sans. Amalaki).
Auri—not yet ; until ; before ; to wait (Sant.).
Āwā—a potter's kiln (Sant., H.).

Āwāj—noise; sound: Syn. Sari (Sant., H.).

Āyo—mother (Sant.).

Āyon }—to wake up.
Eon }

Āyub—evening; nightfall; to cover up by darkness; sunset.

Āyub-jānā—it is evening.

Ayub-mānḍi—evening meal.

Āyub-āyub—5 P.M.

B

Bā—shortened form of Ābā (father).

Bā'—flower (Sant. Bāhā).

Bā—flesh (in the language of children).

Bā—exclamation of surprise or joy.

Ba'-hisir—flower necklace.

Ba'-kobi—cauliflower.

Bābā—paddy (Sant. Hoṛo). Varieties of paddy: Bara-sal, Charki-ras, Goda baba, Jeugne, Kanaow, Karanga, Karanri, Nan-baba, Bai-suri, Rautguli.

Bābā-her-tukām—the ceremony of throwing paddy by bride (which the bride's mother receives on her cloth) as a token of repayment of debt to her parents, before the final departure of the bride after marriage.

Bābāi—to repair.

Ba-bai-ko—builders.

Bābnā—a dwarf (H., Beng., Sans. Bāman).

Bābār—twice (Sant.).

Babatre—on account of; for; regarding; about (H. Bābat).

Bābtā—to itch (B. Baptā).

Bābu—younger brother of the Munda or headman; a male infant.

Bābuān—members of the younger branch of the family of a Munda headman

Bāchāo
Bānchāo } —to save; to protect (H. Bāchānā).

Bāchhā—a bull calf (H.).

Bāchhi—a female calf (H.).

Bāchom—sāboi grass (B. Sāboi, H. Sāboi, Sant. Bāchkom).

Bād—to subtract; to omit.

Bādābādi—to accuse each other; to argue; to contest.

Baḍā
Baṛā } —suffixed to veros to denote moving about, here and there; *e.g.*, Nir-baṛā, Nām-baṛā.

Bāḍā-buḍu—to bubble; to whisper.

Baḍā-giri—to be conceited; vanity; to give oneself an air of superiority.

Baḍ-āi—to be proud (H. Baṛāi).

Bādar—cloudy; the month of Bhādo (*i. e.*, Bhādra).

Bādi
Bāid } —third class low land or Don (Sant. Bād).

Badi—ill-will; enmity (Sant.).

Baḍkao—to increase.

Badlā—exchange; revenge (Sant., H.).

Badnām—bad name; to disgrace (H.).

Bāe—a disease of the nerves; hysteria (H.).

Bāe
Bāihā } —wages paid in kind.

Bāedāsi
Bāihādāsi } —a servant who is paid in kind.

Bāenā—earnest money; advance.

Bāgāhi—dangerous; infested with tigers and leopards.

Bāgān—garden (H., Beng.).

Bāgekedte—leaving out; except.

Bāghāout—spirit of a man killed by a tiger.

Bāghāout bongā—the deity-invoked by those who practice magic. It is believed that they can transform themselves into tiger for the time being and are called Ulaṭ-bāghā or Hoṛo-kulā. Syn. Kulā bongā.

Bagi—a tum tum (H.).

Bāgi / Bāge }—to leave off; to abandon; to give up; to quit; without; except (B. Bāgi).

Bāgichā—garden (H.).

Bāgoā—a short loin cloth worn by old men (H. Kaupin): see also Kupin.

Bāgṛāo—to spoil (H. Bigṛānā, B. Be*n*ṛāo); to commit a mistake.

Bāguli—a purse; a pouch.

Bāh'—bravo; well-done (H.).

Bāhā / Bā' }—flower; to adorn with flowers.

Bāhā-hisir / Ba'-hisir }—flower necklace: see Bā'-hisir.

Bahāl—in good health; to employ; to engage (H.).

Bahāli—appointment.

Bāhānā / Bāhnā }excuse; show; pretence (H.).

Bā'-hāṇḍā—a small pitcher used during the Bā' festival.

Bā' hāṇḍā dā kānāe—*lit.* one fit to carry a small pitcher; a girl aged ten.

Bā'-parab, Bāhā-parab—a festival of the Mundas observed in the month of Chait (April) in celebration of the Vernal Equinox. There is no fixed date for its observance. When the Sal tree blossoms the Pahan worships the Chaṇḍi Bongā in the Jāer Sarnā or Sarhul Sarnā.

Bāhār—outside ; beyond ; to eject ; to get out (H.).

Bahi—book (H.).

Bahilā—barren : Syn. Ṭānṭi (Sant. Bāhlā) (H.).

Bahirā—deaf ; obstinate ; disobedient (H.).

Bahakāo / Phuslāo—to instigate ; to mislead by a false inducement.

Bahlāo—to amuse oneself (H.).

Bahu—younger brother's wife : Syn. Hāgā-kimin (H.).

Bahu ḍuki / Bahumut—diabetes (H. Bahumūtra).

Bāi—to make ; to prepare ; to build ; to create ; to take care of (B., H. Bānāo).

Bāibāite—carefully.

Bāibi—extra ; stranger (H.).

Baid—physician (Sans. Vaidya).

Bāid / Bāji—wager (H.).

Bāid / Bādi—third class low land. See Bādi.

Bāid / Baṛi—flood (H. Bāṛh).

Bai*n*ṭhi—an instrument for cutting vegetables or meat (H.).

Bāioā—it will do ; it is all right.

Bairi—enemy ; ill will (H.).

Bāi-ruṛā—to repair (*lit.* to make back).

Baisākh—the month of Baisākh (April-May).

Baisāo—To establish ; to settle (H.).

Baisi—barren (used contemptuously).

Bāj—trap ; net ; to entrap (H.).

Bājā—musical instrument (H. Bājā) ; straw for twisting into ropes.

Bājāniā—a drummer.

Bājār—market : Syn. Pīṭ (H.).

Bājhāni—net ; a tale-bearer ; a sower of discord (H.).

3

Bajhao—to ensnare ; to entrap (H.).

Bājnā—drum (H.).

Bājrā—a kind of grain (H.).

Bāji—See Bāid.

Bākā—stork ; heron : Syn. Ko (B. Bakli, H. Bagulā).

Bakā—the front portion of the foot (including toe).

Bakānḍā, Bakānṛa, Bakanri }—to talk a talk (B. Bakhānṛ ; H. Baknā, Beng. Bākhāna, Bakā).

Bakhardār—a co-sharer (H.).

Bāklā—bark of a tree (H.).

Bakṛā-kuṛid'—plum. (Sans. Vakrakanṭaka ; H. Bair ; B. Koir).

Bakṛi—compound at the back of a house ; any space near a house hedged round ; to hedge round a space.

Bakṛi—garden (B. Ghornā).

Bakṛi-biur—to hedge round a compound.

Baksis—reward (H.).

Bakulā dāru—bramble bush.

Bal—to pierce with a piece of red hot iron (S.).

Bālā—betrothal ceremony ; procession of the bridegroom's party (B. Bāplā).

Bālā-hāi—a kind of fish.

Bālā-sākā—the relations and friends of the bride or bridegroom ; those who participate in a marriage ceremony are all mutually so addressed by either party.

Balam—spear (H.).

Balam—son's father-in-law (B. Samdhi).

Balbal, Balbaldā }—sweat ; to sweat (B. Redgur) (H.).

Bāle-hon—infant ; youth (Sans. Bāla ; B. Bāle-hopon).

Bāle-hopon—very small children.

Bale-mulu—*lit.* child moon ; third or fourth day after the new moon.

Bālu—mad ; mentally deranged (Sans. Bātula ; H. Boulā).

Bāmṛe—brahmin.
Bān—magic shafts (H., Sant.).
Banāi—noun form of Bāi ; making ; creation ; building (H. Bānāoṭi : Beng. Bānāna).
Bānāgi—noun form of Bāgi ; leaving ; desertion.
Banam—a kind of banjo or fiddle.
Bānḍā—tailless (H., Sant., Beng. Beṅṛe).
Bānḍā-lele }
Bānḍā-siki } —the rainbow.
Bāndā—an embankment (H. Bāndh).
Bāndhā—to mortgage, pawn, or pledge (H., Beng.).
Bānḍo—a wild cat.
Bāndrā—a monkey (H.).
Banduk }
Banduku } —gun (H.).
Bāng—used as prefix denoting 'nothing' (S.).
Bāngāiā—does not exist ; is not present (animate).
Bāng koā—do not exist ; are not present (animate).
Bāni—striped ; squirrel ; to colour ; border of a cloth.
Bānitā-Bongā—the class of spirits requiring propitiation by sacrifice to prevent them from doing mischief.
Bāno—negative of menā ; not to exist ; to be dead ; to be absent.
Bānoā }
Bān-nā } —is not present ; does not exist (inanimate) : *cf.* Hindi Bā=is, and nā=not.
Bāṅṛiā—merchant.
Baṅṛsi }
Bansi } fishing-hook.
Bansi-ḍāng—fishing-rod.
Bāp-purkhā—ancestors (H.).
Bāpuṛi—lowliness.
Bā'-parab—See Bāhā parab.
Bār }
Bāriā } —two.

Baṛā—Suffixed to verbs to mean, about, here and there.

Barābari—equal ; equally (B., H. Barābar).

Baṛbaṛao—to speak unmeaningly.

Barāi—a kind of pulse, *Phaseolus Mungo.*

Baṛāi—a blacksmith ; one who smelts iron : Syn. Lohār (H. Lohār).

Bārān—two (inanimate).

Bārānḍi—any strong wine ; brandy.

Bārānkin—two ; both. **Bārānsā**—twice ; both sides.

Bārduṛiad—a bat (S.).

Bariā—two.

Bari-sākā—swelling in the groin ; bubo.

Bārjiu-ākān—pregnant ; be with child : *lit.* with two lives.

Baṛhi—carpenter (B. Baṛhiamu ; B., H. Baṛhi).

Barkā—a kind of lowland paddy.

Barki—a large-sized wrapper ; cloak.

Baroāṛi—to boast ; to vaunt.

Bār-sā—twice.

Bārsing—two days.

Bāru—a kind of lac-bearing tree, *Schleichera Trijuga* (B. Bāru, H. Kusum).

Bārunḍā—a big frog.

Bāsāng—to boil.

Bāsāng-dā-singi—water-fetching time ; about 4 P.M.

Bāsidā—one day old rice-water.

Bāsilā—adge : Syn. Kisla (H. Basla).

Bātauli
Bādleṭa } —a festival celebrated before any transplantation is done in a Munda village in the month of Āsāṛh (July).

Bāti—a lamp ; a light (H.).

Bāṭijānā
Bāṭinjānā } —to fall on one's back.

Bāṭin—to sleep ; to lie down (B. Giti).

Bāṭikesed'—to obstruct flow of water, by rolling something over an opening.

Batikom—moreover ; often loosely used for 'but' (B.).
Bāu—to rot : Syn. Soyā.
Bāu—elder brother (B. Mārāng dādā ; H. Bhāiā).
Bāu-honjār } —husband's elder brother ; wife's elder
Bāu-hāsur } brother (B., H. Bhaisur).
Bāyār—rope.
Beāj—interest.
Bed'—turban ; to wear a turban ; to tie on the head.
Bedā—to cheat ; to deceive ; deceitful.
Bé-e—to spit (B.).
Bé-dā—saliva.
Begā-ge—quickly ; speedily.
Begār—without (H.).
Bened'—head-dress ; pagri ; turban (B., H. Pāgṛi).
Bengaṛ—brinjal (B. Benghar ; Beng. Begun).
Berā—bracelet ; bangle (B.).
Berej'-jagar—conversation.
Berel—green ; unripe ; uncooked ; raw : Syn. Peṭo (B. Beler).
Berel-berel—quite fresh.
Berel-sud'—leprosy, believed to be caused by the Nāge-erā : Syn. Ārej-gāo.
Beserā—a species of hawk, bigger than the 'Richi.'
Bes—well ; to treat well.
Bes-to—very well.
Betekan—very much (H.).
Beṭ-begāri—personal service in lieu of rent (H.).
Bhadli } —bat (H. Bātuli).
Bhādur }
Bhagat—a witch finder.
Bhāgoā—See Bāgoā.
Bhaiād—agnate relations.
Bhakuā—a fool (H.).
Bhānḍār—treasury ; storehouse.
Bhānḍāri—storekeeper ; steward.

Bhāngrāo—to estrange (H.).

Bhānjāo—to change coins (H. Bhā*n*jāo).

Bhāo—price ; rate (H.).

Bhar—full ; whole (H.)

Bhāṛā—hire (H.).

Bharosā—hope ; expectation (H.).

Bhāṭi—grog shop (H.).

Bhe*n*ṭ—to meet : Syn. Nāpām (B., H.).

Bhogtā—a Bhogtā (a caste).

Bhowrā-inung—a kind of outdoor game.

Bhugut-bāndhā—a form of mortgage in which the loan is repaid by the usufruct of the mortgaged property.

Bhumij—Mundas of the Tamar and Manbhum area.

Bhu*n*s—big rat.

Bhui*n*hār—the name originally given by the Chota Nagpur state to the chiefs of the Mundas, now applied to all descendants of the original Munda settlers and founders of villages.

Bhui*n*hāri—pertaining to Bhui*n*hār ; the land tenure of a Bhui*n*hār.

Bhusṛi—mosquito.

Bhut—spirit.

Bhuti—day labourer.

Bhutkhetā—land set apart for the worship of Bhut or spirit.

Bi'
Biu } —to be satisfied ; to be filled ; to be satiated (after a rice meal).

Biā*n*ṛā—paddy seedling.

Biar-buṭi-bāhā—various kinds of flowers.

Biā*n*ṛ-bakṛi—land for rearing paddy seedlings.

Bichā—to pick up.

Bichār—to judge ; to conclude (H.).

Bid'—to plant in the ground ; to pitch a tent (*cf.* Sans. Biddha).

Bidā—to dismiss; to depart; departure (H.).
Bil—to spread (B. Āṭed').
Bilam—delay : Syn. Heṛā (H.).
Bili—to ripen; egg.

Bili-jitāo } —to be overripe; so as to be unfit for
Jārom-jitāo } consumption.

Bilkā—to be moved with compassion or pity.
Binḍā—a pad of straw to keep pots in position.
Bind-dāru—castor plant: Syn. Jāṛā dāru (B. Jāṛādāru).
Bindram—spider (H., B. Mākṛā).
Bindramjālom—cobweb (B. Mākṛājhāli).
Binḍu—upper ear-ring.
Bing—snake (B., Sant.). Different varieties of snakes: Chiti bing, Dhoria bing, Gāḍā bing (python), Gohmon bing, Jambuṛ bing, Leong bing (non-venomous), Lur bing, Panḍu bing (cobra), Tetria bing.
Bin'ga—to separate; to divide (B., Beng. Bhinna).
Biniur—noun from Biur; crooked; round.
Binji—the Vindhya hills.
Binsāri—early morning dance.
Binti—to beseech; prayer (B., H., Beng. Minati).
Binti hisir—prayer bead.
Bipingā—division.
Bir—a big jungle; a forest.
Biṛā—a bundle of crop.
Biṛā—to beat.
Biṛāo—to tempt; to test; to watch and see.
Birhoṛ—a caste (*lit.* men of the forest).
Birid'—to rise; to get up; to publish; to issue (B.).
Birkeṛā—wild buffalo (B. Sāel).
Birminḍi—bear : *lit.* sheep of the forest (B. Birbuṛhia; Nagpuria Hindi Banbheṛi).

Birni—a wasp (H.).

Bir-renko—wild beast (*lit.* those of the forest).

Birsukuri—wild boar (B.).

Birudh—against (H.).

Bisi—poison (B., Sant., Sans. Visham).

Bisijāng—spine (B.).

Biswās—to believe (H., Beng., Sans.).

Bitar—inside (B., H., Beng. Bhitar).

Biṭi—forced labour (Nagpuria Betbegāri).

Biṭi—a kind of game.

Bitlāo—to annoy; to weary.

Biur—to surround; to turn round; to move round; around.

Biur-bakṛi—See Bakṛi-biur.

Bo—head.

Bo-hāsu—head-ache.

Bo-hāsā—fine earth used as soap.

Bohni—to make the first sale of the day for cash (H., Sant., Pohnā).

Bo jāmbṛā—north.

Bo-jāng—skull.

Bo-kandṛu—south.

Bocho-cheṅṛe—a kind of bird (H., Beng. Pāpiā).

Boḍe, Boḍej', Boḍoe —rice beer: Syn. Ili (H. Pachwāi).

Bode-te, Bode-ge —with great force; speedily.

Bodi—a kind of pulse: Vinga catiang.

Boko, Boko boyā—younger brother (uterine): Syn. Unḍi or Unḍite (B.).

Bolo—to enter (B.).

Bolo-tā-ṭāiād—the place of entrance.

Bonḍol—the end of the boṭoe or loin cloth, which hangs behind.

Bongā—spirit (either good or bad); God, to worship or sacrifice.

Bonolo—entrance; gate.

Bonorsā—hope; expectation.

Bor—bridegroom (H. Bar).

Boṛ—hornet; wasp.

Boṛā—dirty water (B. Poṇḍe).

Bor-āgiā—ceremony of goat sacrifice connected with a marriage ceremony.

Borkod'—lungs (B. Ihim).

Boro—to frighten; to be frightened; fear; fright.

Borsi—fire pan.

Borosoro—fearful; cowardly.

Bortiā—bridegroom's party (H. Barātiā).

Boṭā—the upper part of a hubble-bubble.

Boṭej' } —loin-cloth (B. Karea).
Boṭoe }

Botolo—bottle.

Botong—to frighten (B. Botor).

Bū'—a hole, to make a hole through.

Bū'—bark of a dog (B. Bhu').

Buchā—broken; defective (*cf.* Beng. Bo*n*chā).

Buḍu buḍu—to speak in whispers.

Bugi—to do good; to cure.

Bugin—good; well.

Bugin soāntānā—sweet-scented.

Bugi-bugi—quite well; all right.

Bujāo—to understand; to perceive (H. Bujhnā; Beng. Bujhā).

Bul—to be drunk; drunkard (B.).

Bulā kānā—to get intoxicated.

Bulu—thigh (B.).

Bulung—salt; tasteful (B.).

4

Ḅur—to make a hole (B. Buhr).

Burā—to fill a vessel by dipping into water.

Buṛi—old.

Buṛiā—a bear : Syn. Birmiṇḍi.

Buṛiā—an old woman.

Buṛu—cakes made of pulses (H. Barā ; Beng. Baṛā).

Buṛu—hill ; to heap up ; to hold a fair (because fairs are usually held on hill-tops) ; to call something a mountain (B.).

Buruberạ̄—flat and level land at the foot of a hill.

Burudhasnā—steep slope of a hill.

Buru hāṅgi—a pit at the foot of a hill.

Burum—to lie down (used of animals only) : sometimes used contemptuously of men.

Busu—straw (B.).

Busu gāṇḍu—straw cushion to sit upon.

Buṭā—stem (B. Dāru subā).

Buṭi— { navel.
navel-cord.

Buṭuni—younger sister (B., H. Bahin).

C

Chā—tea.

Chāb—to yawn (B. Chahap).

Chābā—to finish ; end : used as a suffix to verbs to denote completion of an action (Sant.).

Chābḍur—sound made by something falling into water (Sant. Cabhar cabhur).

Chaḍu—to throw into water.

Chakad'—leaven ; sourness ; craftiness.

Chāk—wheel.

Chakad'-te—by false accusation.

Chādrā—cloth sheet.

Chādrā—a bald-headed person (Sant. Caḍṛi).

Chākar—broad (H.) (Sant. Cạnendar).

Chākāting—to mourn : Syn. Hiāting.

Chāki—circular heaps of paddy-bundles (after the harvest).

Chākiāo—to keep paddy in circular heaps.

Chakmak—to shine : Syn. Jhakmakao (H., Beng., Sant.).

Chālā—sieve (H., Beng. Chālni (Sant.).

Chālāo—to set in motion ; to drive ; to manage (H.).

Chālom / Chād'lom }—tail (B. Chānṛ bol).

Chālom-ipil—comet.

Chālu—to dig or turn over the earth of a muddy lowland ; to scrape the ridge of a field.

Chālu-usar—to scrape ; to cut down and extend.

Chānḍā—subscription ; rent ; contribution (H., Beng.).

Chāndāe—the roof projecting beyond the walls ; eaves.

Chandan—sandal ; to paste with sandal (H., Beng.).

Chānḍi-bongā—a village deity of the Mundas worshipped during the Ba'-Parab.

Chānḍi-sarnā—a sacred grove of the village community dedicated to the Chānḍi-bongā.

Chāndi—silver (H.).

Chāonri—a long-tailed cow (H.).

Chānḍu—moon (H. Chānd ; Beng., Sans. Chandra).

Chānḍu—month.

Chāpi—to wash anything ; to wipe off (B.).

Chāpua—bellows (B.).

Chāpu—to examine ; to explore ; to touch in order to feel.

Chāpu-bāṛā—to explore about ; to feel about with the hand (H. Tamarna ; Sant. Tunum).

Chāpud'—husk : Syn. Heṛe.

Chāṛā-chenṛe—a kind of small bird of the sparrow species (H., Beng. Bābui).

Chāṛrā—bald ; baldness.

Chārguṛiā—a drag net.

Chãri—sticks used in sewing up leaves.

Chãri-chãṭãni—one who makes leaf-cups for a Paṛha feast.

Charkhã—a spinning wheel (H., Beng.).

Chãṭkã—a large bamboo basket.

Chãtom—a bamboo umbrella (Beng., Sans. Chhatra).

Chãṭu—earthen pot; pitcher.

Chaudol—litter (Sans. Catur-dola).

Chãuli—rice.

Chãuli-jãng-sagun—divination by the process of 'Selection of rice.'

Chãuli-jãng-sãlãni—one who is skilled in divining causes of illness by the process of 'Selection of rice.'

Chãuli-heper—ceremony of sprinkling rice on the head of the bride.

Chechã—broken or torn; to tear into pieces.

Chelo—kettle.

Chelãng—earthen pot (B. Chatu-tilai).

Chengãhãl—a kind of out-door game.

Chenṛe—bird (Sant.).

Chenṛe-uri, Eṛe-uri—omen consulted before settling a marriage, *e. g.*, the flight of certain birds in certain directions.

Chenṭã—envy; jealousy; cleverness.

Cheped'—to suck; to lick; flat.

Chepo or Cheped—flat (H., Beng. Cheptã).

Chepor—nightingale (B. Jaurhum).

Cheṭ, Cheṭe, Chenṭ—cunning; clever (B. Chirgal; Sans. Cheṭa, sly, deceitful).

Chetãn—upon; above; upper (B.).

Chetãn-guchu—moustache.

Chetão—to advise; to bring to sense (H.).

Cheṭe—See Cheṭ.

Chhamã—to forgive: *cf.* Sans. Kshamã.

Chhati—ceremony observed on the 8th day after the birth of a child (H.).

Chhaṭ-paṭiā—restless (H.).

Chhaṭ-paṭāo—to be restless (H.).

Chhatri—a caste of the Hindus.

Chhipni—plate.

Chhir—udder.

Chhuchi—nose pin.

Chhur—a kind of out-door game.

Chhuṭi—leave ; acquittal ; discharge.

Chi—what, an interrogation suffix.

Chiā—why.

Chiāchi—because.

Chidgi—to stone.

Chikā—or not ; yes or no : He-chikā—Tell me if it is correct or not, yes or no.

Chikāleka—like what ; in what way.

Chikān—what kind ; what sort.

Chikānā—what kind one (inanimate) ? what is it ? what ?

Chikāni—what-kind one (animate) ?

Chikān-king—two of what kind ?

Chikānko—what-kind ones ?

Chilekā—how ; in what way.

Chilkā—how.

Chilekān—what quality ; what description

Chilekān-ā—what-like one (inanimate) ?

Chilekāni—which-like one (animate) ?

Chilekān-king—which-like two ?

Chilekān-ko—which-like ones ?

Chilkān—what sort.

Chilkāte—how ; in what manner.

Chimāe—why (in the language of the poetry).

Chimin—how many (animate).

Chimnāug—how much ; how many (inanimate).

Chimṭā—pincer.
Chimtāng—what time ; when ?
Chinā—what.
Chināmente—what for ; wherefore ; why.
Chingāo—to separate (H. Chhingao).
Chinhā—to recognise : Syn. Nel-uṛung.
Chinhā-parchā—acquaintance : Syn. Nepel-upṛum.
Chini—sugar.
Chipā—to squeeze : Syn. Renḍed', Āinṭhāo.
Chipi—shallow brass dish.
Chiprud'—a flying insect.
Chipud'—a handful.
Chirā—torn ; a portion (B., H.).
Chitar-kābar—spotted (especially red and white).
Chiṭhi—letter (H., Beng.).
Chitirbitir—to scatter ; scattered (H.).
Chitri—partridge (H. Titir).
Chimtā—when.
Chiulāo—ever ; at any time.
Chiulā-o-kā—never.
Cho, Chumān—ceremony of kissing before a marriage (cf. Sans. Chumbana).
Choke—frog (B.).
Cholāng—to scrape out (Beng. Chhoiā ; H. Chhilna).
Chongā—funnel ; a funnel of leaves (Beng.).
Chop—fibre rope.
Chopod', Cheped'—to suck.
Choṭā-bā—a kind of flower.
Chowrā—third class low land.
Chu, Cho—to kiss (B., H., Beng. Chumā ; Sans. Chumbana).
Chui, Chuihon—calf.

Chuchundar—musk rat: Syn. Chundi (B.).

Chuk—a mistake; to mistake (*cf.* Beng. Bhul-chuk).

Chukā—a small earthen pot.

Chukuri—circular rain hat made of leaves.

Chumān } —kissing ceremony performed as a preliminary to
Cho } a marriage ceremony; blessing the bridal pair.

Chulhā—hearth (Beng. Chulā).

Chunā—lime.

Chunāuti—a small wooden box for keeping powdered lime.

Chundi—pig-tail; musk rat (S. Chund).

Chunḍul—to point out with the finger.

Chunḍul-ḍāḍo—the pointing finger or forefinger.

Chunḍul-sārsār—the nail of the pointing finger, loosely used for the forefinger.

Chupād'—bush.

Churin—a kind of malevolent spirit or bongā (H.).

Churlā—glass armlet (H., Beng. Churi).

Chuṭā—tobacco rolled up in a leaf; cigarette (Sant. Cuṭi).

Chuṭā } —tuft of hair on the crown of the head
Chuṭā-ub' } (B. Churchutia: *cf.* Beng. Jhunṭi).

Chuṭi—the point at the top of anything.

Chuṭu—mouse (smaller species) (Sant. Cutia).

D

Dā—give me.

Dā-ā'—elder brother (vocative).

Dā—water; rain (Sant. Dak') (B.)

Dā-horo—tortoise.

Dā-mānḍi—food and water (Sant. Dak' daka).

Dā-sim—water fowl.

Dā-sonsore—grasshopper living in water.

Dā-āu-ni—water-carrier; one who brings water.

Dā-āu—a special ceremony connected with marriage. Four maidens go out to a neighbouring pond or stream and bring water from it to the bride's house (*cf.* Bengali custom of Jal-sādhā.)

Dāb'—hastily ; quickly ; suddenly.

Dāb—to thatch ; to cover with tiles (B.).

Dab-ruāṛ—to repair a hut (B.).

Ḍābāḍubu—sound of splashed water made when swimming (Saut.).

Ḍabaḍubu—motion of child learning to walk (Sant. Ḍagar-ḍugur).

Dābdābā—influential ; influence.

Ḍābāk-ḍubuk—to sink and rise again (Sant.).

Ḍabal—corrupt form of the English word Double ; a great quantity.

Dābāo—to press down ; to suppress ; to threaten (Sant.).

Ḍābāo—to cover ; to pervade.

Ḍābar—a large rice field (Sant.).

Dā-bāsāngsingi—afternoon, 4 P.M. : *lit.* the time when water is heated for cooking rice for the night meal.

Ḍabḍabāo—to be filled with tears (Sant.).

Dābi—claim ; to claim (Sant., H., Beng.).

Dābi—shoulder blade (Sant.).

Dabkāo }
Dabrāo } —to lie in wait; to crouch down in fear (Sant.).

Ḍabkāo—to boil.

Ḍābni—a covering dish.

Ḍābrāo—to cover ; to spread over (Sant. Dambrao).

Dābruṛā—to repair : *lit.* to cover again.

Dāchā—flag.

Dāchābid'—to plant a flag (*e.g.*, to give delivery of possession of lands, etc.).

Dāchābinid'—planting of a flag.

Dā-chāṭu—water pot ; earthen vessel for holding water.

Daimudai—complainant and accused.

Dādā—elder brother (B.).

Dādāl—reduplication of Dāl ; to strike repeatedly.

Ḍāḍkā—a wooden vessel used for feeding cattle (Sant. Ḍaka-dak).

Dādni—to advance money ; money given in advance.

Ḍāḍo—a species of black ant with a large head ; a big-headed man.

Ḍaḍo—finger ; legs of a crab (Sant. Ḍaṭo ; B., H. Angur from Sans. Anguli).

Ḍāḍu
Ḍāṛu } —big-headed (Sant. Ḍaṭhu).

Dāg
Dāgi } —spot ; blemish (Sant.).

Dāg'—a corruption of 'dā-ā'' meaning water, used as a name-ending of villages, *e.g.*, Hutubdāg, Jamua-dāg, Lohardāga.

Dāgā—to cheat ; to deceive (Sant., H.).

Dāgābāj—deceitful (Sant., H.).

Ḍāgar-ḍāgar—shaking of a large body.

Ḍagḍag—deep red colour.

Ḍagḍagāo—to grow luxuriantly; to burn with a flame (Sant.)

Dāgi—See Dāg.

Dāgimārā—Uri-bulls branded with red-hot iron (these are not used by the Mundas for ploughing).

Dāgni—branding iron.

Dāgul-dāgul—shaggy ; long-haired.

Ḍah'—enmity ; envy ; ill-will (Sant.).

Dāhā—edible roots (Sant. Dā).

Dāhā—bee-hive ; wasp-hive (B. Dā).

Ḍāhāng
Dāng } —a long bamboo, or a long stick.

Ḍahar—path ; track (H.).

Ḍābi—revengeful.

Dahi—curd (H.).

Ḍahi—jhuming.

Dāhināo—to leave off some space to the right and moving to the left while ploughing.

Dāhirchi—to sprinkle water; the ceremony of welcome to the bridegroom in the house of the bride.

Dah-lāo—to wet (Sant.).

Dahlāo—to shake; to quake.

Ḍāhnga—very long; a Mundā sept.

Ḍahrāo—to drive cattle.

Ḍahu—a kind of sour fruit.

Dāi—elder sister (Sant., B.)

Dāi—midwife (Sans. Dhātrī).

Ḍāin—witch: Syn. Najom.

Ḍāiṅṛi—seed separator.

Dāka-dāki } —to push one another.
Dhāka-dhāk

Dākdākāo—to burn with a flame.

Ḍākeḍāk—to convey anything from stage to stage (Sant.).

Dakhal—possession (H.).

Dakhal nām—to take possession.

Dākhil—to pay; to deposit.

Dākhilā—receipt: Syn. Rasdi (Sant.).

Dakhin—south (Sant., Sans., Beng., H.).

Dakhnāhi—southern (Sant., H.).

Ḍāk-oṛā—post-office.

Ḍāku—robber (H.).

Dāl—to beat; to strike; to assault.

Ḍālā—basket (Sant., Beng., Sans. Ḍallakam).

Dālob-dālob—to trot.

Dālāl—a broker, a tout (H.).

Dālān—a mud or brick wall; a brick building (H.).

Ḍālāng-ḍulung—paddy of weak growth; to walk like a sick man.

Dal-dal—marsh; swampy ground (Sant. Dalabi).

Daldal—to shiver (Sant. Daldalāo).
Dāl-i—one fit to be beaten.
Dāli—peas, pulses, split into two pieces (B.).
Ḍāli—basket without lid (Sant. Dalich) (B., Beng.).
Dalidar—voracious.
Ḍālikāṭāri—(from Ḍāli, the Pahan's winnowing fan, and Kāṭāri, the Pahan's sacrificial knife) the service land of the Pahan for priestly service in the village.
Dalil—document (H.).
Dalkāo—to shake.
Dālob—to cover ; to thatch a roof.
Dālui-dālui—long-haired.
Dām—price (H.).
Damā—asthma.
Ḍāmāḍol—to be in trouble.
Damas, Dhamas—a kind of skin disease.
Ḍāmbhā—a pommelo (H.).
Dāmṛā—an earthen lamp.
Dāmṛi—a half-pice.
Dāmul—exile (H.).
Dān—gift ; alms (Sans. Dāna).
Dānā, Dāin, Dā*n*ṛā—to search about.
Dānā—grain ; gram (H.).
Dānāb—covering of a roof ; thatch.
Dānae—to judge.
Dānāis—opinion ; judgment.
Danalob—covering.
Dānāng—to hide from view, to disappear behind ; to die (Sant. Danan).
Dānāpāni—food and drink.

Dānāpāl—covering (from Dapal, to cover).

Dānāpāl—beating; assault (from Dapal, to beat each other).

Ḍanḍ—fine; punishment (Sans. Daṇḍa).

Ḍānḍā—stick; club (H.).

Dāndā—to be surprised (*cf.* Ākādāndā).

Ḍānḍā—waist; loin (H.).

Dāndāgiṛi—to be completely surprised.

Dandanāo—quickly; to walk proudly.

Dāndāti—offerings made to appease a *Bhut* or spirit.

Dā*n*dhā } —occupation; to search; to labour.
Dhāndā }

Ḍanḍe—to impose a fine (Sant. Ḍanḍom; Sans. Daṇḍa).

Ḍāṇḍi—a small stick; balance.

Ḍā*n*ḍikā—a kind of fish.

Ḍānḍom } —a handle.
Dānom }

Ḍāng—bamboo pole; a measure of time: *e.g.*, Mid ḍāng singie rakab kana—The sun rose one ḍāng, *i.e.*, 7 A.M.

Dāng—certainly; of course.

Dāngāhāngāmā—affray; fight (H.).

Dāngi—to rock a child to soothe it.

Dāngṛā } —servant; unmarried boy (Sant. Ḍangua).
Dhāngṛā }

Dā*n*gṛi } —maid servant; unmarried girl (B. Dhangṛin).
Dhāngṛi }

Dā*n*o-dā*n*o—To proclaim; to publish (Sant. Dae-dae).

Dāo*n*ṛi—cattle used for threshing grain (Sant. Dahin).

Dāo*n*ṛi-te-en—threshing by cattle, as opposed to threshing by feet (Kāṭā-te-en).

Ḍā*n*ṛ—upland: Syn. Piṛi.

Dā*n*ṛā—to search; to enquire; to seek (B., Sans. Ḍhun ḍhanam; H. Dhu*n*ṛna).

Dā*n*ṛā-bāṛā—to search about: Syn. Nāmbāṛā.

Dānṛe—offering ; to sacrifice (Sant. Dare) ; sacrificial victim.

Dānṛeyā—to refuse to eat and express dissatisfaction. After a marriage ceremony is over there is a feast in which the bridegroom and his party take part. Nobody may partake of any food until the bridegroom begins to eat. The bridegroom usually refuses to eat until some suitable gift is promised by the father-in-law. The bridegroom is then said to be 'dānṛeyā.'

Ḍānṭā } —stick : Syn. Soṭā
Ḍānḍā }

Dānṭāo—to rebuke.

Ḍānṭi—handle ; stalk (B. Benṭ).

Ḍānṛkā—a kind of fish.

Dāo—opportunity (Sant.).

Dāoghāṭ—to lie in wait.

Dāpā dāpā—sound made by the flapping of wings of birds (used as a verb also).

Dāpāl—reciprocal form of Dāl ; to strike each other.

Dāpāl—a covering.

Dāpālgopoe—a riot ; an affray : a deadly affray.

Dāprom—reciprocal form of Dārom ; to meet each other; the ceremony connected with the first meeting of the bridegroom's party and the bride's party.

Dar—trench ; a line of raised earth for the purpose of sowing.

Ḍār—big branch of a tree (Sant., H., Beng. Ḍāl) : Syn. Ḍārā.

Daram } —religion (H.).
Dharam }

Daram kāji—religious instructions.

Dārāng—to pray and make promises of offerings to a spirit.

Ḍarāo—to frighten (H.).

Daurā—a big basket.

Daurā-dauri—quickly.

Daurāhā—runner.

Daurāo—to send one running ; to chase.

Dauri—a basket.

Dāuri } —to run.
Dhāuri

Dāwā—claim : Syn. Dābi.

Dāwāi—medicine : Syn. Rānu.

Dawāt—inkpot.

Dayā—mercy ; pity.

Ḍayak'-ḍayak'—to trot.

De—interjection.

Deāo—to cause to give ; to compel to pay : Syn. Om-tukā (H. Diladena).

De-e' } —to climb ; to enter a carriage ; to ride on a horse (B.).
Dej'

Ḍebel—to swim (B., H. Pāerna) : Syn. Oiyār.

Ḍebeḍebe—foul water ; muddy water.

Ḍeḍgej'—dwarf.

Ḍegāo—jump ; to cross by jumping over.

Ḍegāo-ene—an out-door game.

Deh—body : Syn. Hoṛmo.

Dehāt—country (H.).

Dej'—See De-e'.

Dekhāo—to show : Syn. Udub'.

Delā—come along (vocative singular, used interjectionally).

Delābu—come along (we all) following me.

Delāng—come along (you and I) (B. Dolang).

Ḍel-ḍel } —a big-bellied person ; applied to a pregnant woman also.
Dil-ḍil

Ḍembā } —clod.
Dhembā

Ḍembo—said of paddy which has not yet grown out of the stalk.

Ḍemchu—a kind of black bird.

Ḍemkā—dwarf and big bellied.

Ḍeṇḍe—tailless ; hairless ; leafless.

Ḍenebel—swimming.

Dengā—to assist ; to help.

Ḍengā—under-cloth put on by a woman when in menses.

Denengā—assistance ; help.

Depengā—reciprocal form of Dengā ; to help each other.

Deo—deity ; spirit ; Syn. Bongā (H.)

Deor—husband's younger brother (H.)

Deonṛā—a witch-finder ; magician ; Syn. Māti, Sokhā (B.).

Deothan—a festival of the Mundas—borrowed from the Hindus.

Depeṛ } —reciprocal form of Deṛ.
Depeṛe }

Deṛ—to copulate (Sant., B. Optong).

Ḍerā—camp ; lodging ; Syn. Ḍerā Oṛā.

Derāng—perhaps ; probably (B., Ja., Sant. Menā).

Der } —delay ; to be late ; Syn. Heṛā (H., Beng.).
Deri }

Ḍeṛ } —one and a quarter ; 50 per cent.
Ḍeṛhi }

Deṛe—same as Depeṛ.

Derej'-derej'—playfully ; in a jocular manner.

Ḍeṛhi—a loan at 50 per cent. interest.

Des—country ; Syn. Disum (Beng., H., Sans. Deśa).

Desāuli bongā—a village deity presiding over the Desāuli sarnā.

Ḍeṭ'-ḍeṭ'—small ; thin.

Dewān—manager (H.)

Dewāni—civil (H.)

Ḍhā—sound of some thing falling.

Ḍhābā—veranda.

Ḍhāḍos—fearless ; brave.

Ḍhāḍra M. }
Ḍhāḍri F. } —old and lean (used contemptuously).

Ḍhāḍri—any old animal (female) (used contemptuously).

Dhāi—a kind of plant.

Dhāk }
Dhāp } —heat ; flame.

Dhākā—to push (H.)

Dhakchakāo }
Dhukchukāo } —to hesitate.

Dhākadhāki—to push each other (H.)

Ḍhākāo—to cover.

Ḍhāki—a large basket.

Ḍhāklāḍhākli }
Ḍheklāḍhekli } —to push each other (H.)

Ḍhāl—shield (H.)

Dhāmādhur—pompously.

Dhamak }
Dhamas } —influence.

Dhamas—a kind of skin disease.

Dhamkāo—to threaten ; to chide (B., Beng., H.).

Dhamkā-dhamki—to threaten (H.).

Dhāmpā-dhompo }
Jhāmpā-jhompo } —cluster of fruits.

Dhamsāo—to beat severely.

Dhāndhā }
Dāndhā } —occupation.

Dhandanāo }
Banbhanāo } —to buzz, as a fly.

Dhāndra-dhundru—Short-sighted.

Ḍhāngā M. }
Ḍhangi F. } —tall.

Dhangar
Dangar
Dhani } —rich ; wealthy (H., Sans., Beng. Dhanī).

Dhāngaṛ—servant.

Dhania—coriander seed (H., Beng.).

Ḍhanmanāo—to fall down.

Ḍhā*n*plā—a kind of drum ; tambourine.

Dhāoā—to go in crowds ; to go in large number.

Dhāo
Dhā*n*o } —time (H.).

Dhāp—flame.

Dhār—debt (H., Beng.).

Dhār—edge (Beng., H.).

Dhārā—flow of water.

Dhāṛā—anything put on a scale to balance equally (H., Beng.).

Dharā-dhari—to catch each other ; hustling.

Dharamḍāk—last warning.

Dhārāo—to be in debt ; to owe.

Ḍharas—patience ; free from fever ; beyond danger.

Ḍharkāo—slope ; to pour out.

Dharmo—true ; truth.

Dharmokāji—true statement.

Dhārnā—to sit at one's door till a prayer is granted (H., Beng.).

Dharnā—the large beam which supports the ridge pole of a roof.

Dharpā—trap.

Dharti—universe ; the earth ; Syn. Ote-disum (Sans. Dharitrī).

Dhasāo—to collapse ; to fall down ; to pull down (H.).

Dhasnā—a pit ; a pit near the slope of a hill.

Ḍhāṭā ḍhuṭu—stumps of trees.

Dhāting—sound of dumāng or drum.

Ḍhāṭkā—twigs of trees.

Dhātu—minerals.

Dhāwādhāwi—to go in a large body.

Ḍhebā M. }—short-statured.
Ḍhebi F.

Ḍheb-ḍhebe }—big-bellied.
Ḍhebrā

Ḍhebuā—pice; money; generally meaning 'two pice.'

Dhejrāhā }—ugly; dirty.
Dhejgar

Ḍhekār—to belch.

Ḍhelā—clod of earth; a kind of thorny plant (H.).

Ḍhelkusi—a sling used to throw stones to a great distance.

Ḍheṅki—husking mortar (H.).

Ḍhenkok'—cry of peacock.

Ḍher—many; much (H.).

Ḍheṛ—a heap (H.).

Ḍherā—a hand spindle.

Ḍhes—to implicate.

Ḍhesā-ḍhesi—to excuse oneself and implicate another (Sant.).

Dhiāputā—family.

Ḍhil }—loose; to neglect (H., Beng.).
Ḍhilāng

Ḍhilāo—to neglect; careless.

Ḍhilisili—careless; lazy (H.).

Ḍhiluā—a swing; to hang; Syn. Hākā.

Ḍhimsi—a big-bellied woman.

Ḍhimā—mild (H.).

Ḍhinḍhi—a pod of cotton.

Ḍhingur—a piece of wood suspended on the neck of cattle so that they may not run away; Syn. Ṭaku.

Ḍhirāo—to threaten (H.).

Ḍhiri }—a heap (H.).
Ḍheri

Dhirisusti—slowly (H.).

Ḍhismis—to dismiss a case ; corrupt form of the English word 'dismiss.'

Ḍhiṭ—obstinate ; impudent (H.).

Ḍhiṭhāi—impudence (H.).

Ḍhoāo—to carry.

Ḍhoṛo—hollow in a tree (H.).

Ḍhodṛo—fat.

Dhokhā—doubt ; to deceive (H.).

Ḍhol—drum.

Ḍholki—a smaller kind of drum.

Ḍholo—a fat and lazy woman.

Ḍholomolo }—drowsy.
Ḍulumulu

Dhomok-chomok—to walk quickly.

Ḍhomsā-ḍhumsi—to walk stumbling.

Ḍhomsol—fat (used contemptuously).

Ḍhonḍ—a man with a long neck.

Dhonḍ }—a kind of snake.
Ḍunḍu

Ḍhopso }—lazy.
Ḍhoso

Ḍhoreā—heat.

Ḍhoṛhā—rivulet ; streamlet (H.).

Ḍhoṛhā—belly (used contemptuously).

Ḍhoṛori }—a kind of tree ; a lean and old woman
Ḍuḍṛi

Ḍhoso—lazy.

Dhoti—cloth (H.).

Dhoān—incense (H.).

Dhubghās—kind of grass (Sans. Dūrvā ; H. Dub).

Ḍhubi—washerman (H.).

Dhukā—storm.

Dhukā-dhuki—to fan.

Dhukāo—to blow bellows ; Syn. Sipud'.

Dhukchukāo—to hesitate ; to be frightened.

Dhuk-dhuk }—to palpitate ; to throb.
Dhuk-dhuki

Ḍhukni—an unmarried woman who forces herself on a man to marry him.

Dhukuchuku—doubtful.

Ḍhulā—a bundle of rope.

Ḍhulki—a kind of small drum ; a fat girl.

Dhum—crowd.

Dhumā M. }—fat and dwarf.
Dhumi F.

Dhumdhām—pomp and display (H.).

Dhumṛā M. }—stout ; fat.
Dhumṛi F.

Dhumur-rasi—honey of the bee of the Dhumur species.

Dhumur-dā—beehive of the bee of the Dhumur species.

Dhumur-engā—a species of small bee called Dhumur.

Dhunāo—to card cotton ; to strike with the horn.

Dhuṅā—smoke ; Syn. Sukul (H., B., Sans. Dhūma).

Dhund—fog ; misty.

Dhundur—smoky

Dhundhā }—short-sighted.
Dundā

Dhundur-musā—dejected ; sad.

Dhungiā—smoke.

Dhungiākān—smoky.

Dhuniā—one who cards cotton.

Ḍhuṅṛa-ḍhuṅṛi—to search about.

Ḍhuṅṛāo—to search (H. Dhuṅṛnā ; Sans. Ḍhunḍhaṇam).

Dhup—heat of the Sun (H.).

Dhupdhuman—incense (H.).

Dhur
Dhurā } —dust ; to beat into powder.
Dhuṛi

Dhurdhurāo—to hate ; to drive out contemptuously.

Dhuriāo—to collect ; to gather.

Dhurjhārāoni—fee paid for cleansing one's feet which is covered with dust.

Dhurmār—to hate.

Dhurut—clever ; a cheat ; Syn. Chenṭ.

Dhusā—a kind of woollen cloth.

Dhusāo
Dusāo } —to blame, to dislike.

Dhut—interjection ; to signify annoyance or contempt.

Ḍi
Ḍih' } —village ; *Basti* ; hamlet.

Dia
Dimi } —lamp.

Diāsalāi—matches (H.).

Ḍibi—a small earthen vessel.

Ḍiḍi—to stand (said of children).

Ḍidi—a vulture.

Ḍiḍin—to stand on tip-toe.

Ḍiḍgar—fearless.

Ḍiḍ—to be firm ; to take courage.

Ḍigao—to remove ; to move.

Ḍigimigi
Ḍagmagāo } —to shake.

Ḍigir-ḍigir—to shake.

Ḍigri—a decree ; corrupt form of the English word 'decree.'

Diguār—a Chaukidar ; rural Police.

Diguāri—pertaining to a Diguār.

Ḍihāri—pertaining to a Ḍi.

Ḍihāri-kore—round about the village.

Dik
Dik-dik } —annoyance (H.).

Dikdikao—to annoy.

Dikiāo—to annoy.

Diku—a high-caste foreigner, as opposed to Kero—a low caste foreigner ; a land-lord.

Diku—language of a foreigner.

Dikuntānā—to show one's superiority ; to lord over.

Dikuperā—a foreigner guest.

Dil—mind (H.).

Ḍilḍāl—swaying motion.

Ḍil-ḍil—pregnant.

Ḍili
Ḍhili } —to loosen ; to slacken.

Ḍili—a large basket.

Dilgar
Dilwār
Ḍiḍgar } —brave ; bold.

Ḍilkāo—to throw down by beating gently.

Dimāk—pride (H.).

Dimāki—proud.

Ḍimbā-poṭā—the upper intestine.

Ḍimbu—a kind of fruit.

Dimiḍānḍi—lamp-stand.

Ḍimni—a large basket for storing grain.

Din—day ; Syn. Hulāng (H.) ; Tamaṛia Mundari Syn. Dilā (H.).

Dināki—daily ; every day (H.).

Dinbhar—whole day ; Syn. Singiburā, or Singisāṭuh.

Ḍinḍā—virgin ; unmarried ; barren (H.).

Din-ete—since the day.

Ḍingiḍāngā—to swing to and fro.

Ḍingṛā—dwarf and roundish.

Dinihār
Dāni } —liberal ; generous (H.).

Dipli—time; moment; instant; season.

Ḍipu—corrupt form of the English word 'Depôt.'

Diremonte—in calmness of mind.

Ḍiṛh—firm; Brave.

Diri—stone.

Diring—horn.

Dirisehel—a stone mortar.

Disā—side; direction (H.).

Disi—native; country-made (H., Beng.).

Ḍismis / **Ḍhismis**—corrupt form of the English word 'Dismiss.'

Distā / **Jistā**—one quire (H., Beng.).

Disum—country (Sans. Deśa).

Do—to place; to keep; to keep in concubinage. Sometimes loosely used to mean marriage in Sagai form (B. Dohoe).

Do—too; then; affixed to words to emphasise, *e.g.*, Amdo, Aedo, Nado, Mendo.

Doāt—inkpot (H., Beng.).

Dobar—double; twice as much (H.).

Ḍobe—to dip in water.

Ḍobhā—pond (H.).

Ḍobo—drowsy: to nod the head as a sign of consent (B. Duṛum).

Ḍobol-ḍobol—heaving up and down on the surface of water (Sant. Dombol-dombol).

Dobrāo—to fold; to plough for the second time; to repeat.

Dodād'—to deny (Sant. Dodao).

Dodhāri—two-edged (H.).

Ḍoḍo / **Ḍuki**—to urinate; urine (B. Aru).

Ḍoḍom-ḍoḍom—to walk with shaking of the head (as of old and aged persons).

Do-eme—keep it (inanimate).

Doime—keep it (animate).

Dogā—come! same as Do.

Ḍohā-bohā—to carry away (Dhona).

Dohāe—to appeal; to cry for help (H., Beng.).

Dohār—a water channel for letting out water from a Bāndh.

Dohmat—to blame; blame (H.).

Doho }
Do } —to keep: see Do.

Doi—to sit, in the language of children (also used when addressing children). Shortened form of Dub.

Dohrāo—to double up; to plough for the second time; to repeat.

Doj'—parrot: Syn. Miru.

Ḍokā—a kind of tree.

Ḍokā }
Bokā } —an idiot.
Kokā }

Dokān—shop (H.).

Dokāndār—shopkeeper (H.).

Dokhā }
Dhokhā } —to cheat; disappointment; doubt.

Ḍokod'-ḍokod'—slack; loose.

Dokhol—to occupy; occupancy; possession (H., Beng. Dakhal).

Dokrā—a half-pice.

Dol—the Hindu festival.

Ḍol—iron bucket.

Dolā—exhortative particle signifying 'Come; Come on.'

Dolā }
Dogā } —come; let us go.
Delā }

Dolābu—come; let us all go.

Dolāng—Come; let us go (you and I).

Ḍolāo—to shake; to ring the bell (H.).

Ḍol-ḍāl—to stagger.

Doloe-doloe }
Dalae-dala^{e} } —to walk with loosened hair waving in the wind.

Ḍoli—a sort of palanquin (H., Beng. Ḍooli).

Dolop′-dolop′ }
Julup-julup } —flickering unsteadily.

Ḍom—a low-caste aboriginal tribe.

Ḍomṛā—a defiled and outcasted man.

Ḍomṭunki—basket.

Don—low land for growing paddy.

Dondo—to raise up.

Ḍonḍo—fool; foolish; ignorant (B., Beng. Bokā).

Ḍongā—a boat.

Dongol—fire : Syn. Sengel.

Dopo }
Dopho } —reciprocal form of Do; to love each other.

Ḍorābing—a kind of snake (B. Dorabing).

Dorob—ornaments; valuable articles.

Dorobos—all; ruin.

Dorogā—a head constable, or sub-inspector of police.

Do-rasā—mixed (used of tobacco only).

Dos—sin; fault : Syn. Gunha (H., Beng.).

Dosimāni—boundaries of two villages (H.).

Doskhot—signature; to sign.

Doyā—back.

Doyā-e-me—turn your back and follow me.

Doyāhisā—hinder part; back part; latter part.

Duān }
Dumān } —raisin (B., H., Beng. Dhunā).

Duār—door (H., Beng.).

Duārsini—door silt.

Dub′—to sit.

Dubā-cheṛe—a kind of bird.

Ḍubāo—to immerse in water: Syn. Ḍumbui.

Dubākān—sitting; assembled.

Ḍubhā—a kind of brass cup.

Ḍubhi }
Ḍubri } —a small brass cup.

Dudmul—pigeon.

Dudub' }
Dunub' } —a sitting; a meeting.

Ḍudugar—foggy; misty; smoky (either on account of smoke or on account of fog).

Dudul—act of pouring out.

Ḍugur-ḍugur—to walk very slowly.

Ḍui—to catch fish by stirring up the water so that fishes come out on the surface.

Ḍuki—to urinate; urine (B. Aru).

Ḍukipoṭom—one who always urinates; a term of abuse.

Duku—trouble; sorrow; pain; illness (H. Dukh; Beng., Sans. Dukhaḥ).

Dul—to pour something.

Dulāṛ—to love; darling; dear.

Duldā—ceremony of pouring consecrated water on the bridal pair.

Duldulāo—luxuriant.

Ḍulu—a leap cup: Syn. Kui (Sant. Ḍolkha).

Ḍulumulu—sad looking; dejected (Sant. Dolomolo).

Dumāng—a drum.

Dumbu—grass.

Ḍumbui—to immerse in water; to sink.

Dundu—an owl of the big species.

Dundur—indistinctly visible; defective eyesight.

Dundu-ene }
Dundu-inung } —the game of blind man's buff.

Ḍunḍṛāo—to search about for anything (H. Ḍhunṛnā; Sans. Dhunḍhanam).

Ḍunḍu-bing—a kind of snake (B.).

Ḍungā—to suspend; to hang; to carry by hanging: Syn. Hākā (B. Jhulā).

Duniā—world.

Dupul—reciprocal form of Dul.

Ḍur—a kind of bird.

Durā—door; dust.

Durāng—song; to sing. Varieties of songs are: Genā, Jādur, Jāpi, Jārgā, Karam, Lahsuā, Māge.

Ḍuriā—plaited thread (false hair).

Dursut—to put right.

Duṛum—to lie down and sleep.

Durumusu—ill; indisposed (Sant. Dodorso).

Dusman—enemy (H.).

Dutām—negotiator in a marriage.

E

E—vocative.

E—abbreviated form of third personal pronoun.

E—lac (B.).

E }
Eā } —seven.

E-ābā—oh father (a form of address used by children).

Eām—to cry; to weep.

Eāngā—oh mother (a form of address used by children).

Ebe-tebe—same as Ābe-tābe.

Eḍe-beḍe }
Enḍe-benḍe } —a confused statement.

Edel—cotton; cotton trees; *Bombax malabaricum* (Semar., Beng. Simul).

Eee′ }
Ij′ } —stool (B.).

Eger—to abuse; to quarrel; to chastise.

Ejāhār
Ijāhār } —deposition.

Ejāhār-omjādā—gave evidence.

Ejlās
Ijlās } —court.

Ejmāl
Ijmāl } —joint: Syn. Mid're.

Ekā—alone: Syn. Eskār.

Ekālte—at once; instantly: Syn. B. Odege or Bodete.

Ekbārgi
Ekdom } —entirely: Syn. Misātorsā.

Eklā—to shake; to quake; to quiver; to tremble; to move.

Ekrār—to agree; to promise.

Ekrārnāmā—agreement.

Eksātte—together: Syn. Midte.

Ektiār—authority; control.

Ektorpha—one-sided; ex-parte.

Elā—exclamation; calling one's attention; come.

Elākā
Ilaka } —country; province; jurisdiction: Syn. Simān, Disum.

Elāng—let us go (two of us).

Elāng—to give out heat.

Ele-ele—in a light manner; jestingly.

Em—abbreviated form of 'Om.'

Em
Om } —to give.

Emruṛā
Om-ruāṛ } —to give back.

Emānko—et cetera; such ones.

En—that (adj.) (inanimate and animate).

En—to thresh by treading with feet.

En-utār—to thresh out completely (utār—suffix to denote completion of an action).

Ena—that one (inanimate).

Enādo—that one (pointing out the object).

Enādo—then ; thereupon.

Enāge—that one ; that's it.

Enāng—then ; at that time. A suffix indicating a past hour within the day.

Enāo—that also.

Enāmente—for that reason ; therefore.

Enāmentedo—therefore.

Enāre—if that be so.

Enḍā—to throw.

Endrej'—four days hence.

Enej', **Ene**—game; Syn. Inung.

Eneṭej'—beginning.

Engā—mother ; added to words to denote the female sex.

Engā-āpu—parents.

Engā-bāge-lijā—the cloth given to the mother of the bride.

Engājopor, **Engājukur**—*lit.* fit to be a mother; a woman aged 20 to 25.

Engākaṭu—the big toe.

Enreo, **Iminreo**—even if ; even then.

Engāsārsār—the middle finger.

Engāṭepo—thumb.

Engel-pengel—topsyturvy ; to turn on the sides.

Enkā—like that.

Enkāte—in that way ; in that manner.

Enko, Inko—those.

Enlekā—like that.

Enpārom—beyond that.

Enre—in that ; there.

Enredo, Kāredo—otherwise, or else ; but then.

Eṛen, Enṛen—to quench ; to extinguish (B. Inri).

Ensā, Ensāre—on that side.

Entāre—in that place ; on that side.

Entāiomte—after that ; subsequently ; thereafter.

Ente—there ; by that ; then.

Eon—to awake ; to wake up.

Eotrong—a kind of fruit (H. Kari).

Epegār, Eperāng—reciprocal form of Eger, and Erang ; quarrel dispute ; bad terms.

Eplāng—to bask in the sun.

Erā—a full-grown woman.

Eṛāge—certainly ; much.

Erāng—to abuse ; to chastise ; to quarrel ; to scold.

Eṛe-uri—auspicious omen.

Esānḍi—wooden frame of a plough.

Esed'—to be angry ; dissatisfied.

Esel—rain ; white.

Eskār—alone ; only one ; lonely (H. Ekelā ; Beng. Ekā).

Eskarge—alone (emphatic).

Eṭā—another ; a different ; other.

Eṭā-gā—another thing (inanimate).

Eṭā-hulā—another day.

Eṭā-king—two other (animate).

Eṭā-ko—others ; other ones (animate).

Eṭā-ni—another one (animate).

Etāng—thin ; fine.

Etbār—to believe.

Ete—from (Beng. Haite).

Eṭe—to begin.

Eṭed'—to feel uneasy ; to feel tired.

Eṭej'—beginning.
Etel—to aim.
Eṭem-ṭerem—many things; miscellaneous things.
Eṭkā—to be bad.
Eṭkān—bad, evil.
Eṭkānhāsā—bad soil.
Eṭkān-ṭāiād—dirty place.
Etong—to retort quickly.
Etwār—Sunday.

G

Gā-ā'—to sew up mats.
Gābhā—middle; pith (Sant., H., Sans. Garbha).
Gachāo—to promise; to undertake (Sant., H.).
Gāchi—plants (Sant., H.).
Gāḍā—river.
Gāḍābing—snake living in water.
Gādar—to be full-grown; just before ripening.
Gādar } —half ripe.
Gādra }
Gādhā—ass; donkey.
Gāḍhā-goḍho—up and down; rough.
Gādi—dumb.
Gādla—unclean.
Gāgrā—water pot: Syn. Dāchāṭu.
Gahnā—ornament.
Gāi—cow.
Gāi-horā—the milky way (Sant. Panjar dahar).
Gāi-uri—cows.
Gaj—measuring rod; one yard.
Gaj' gaj'—difficulty; trouble; inconvenience.
Gālāng—to make mats by inter-twining the palm leaves.

Gālāng-kārdhāni—a belt made of plaited thread; to bind hair with tape.

Gālāo—to melt: Syn. Ser.

Gāli—to abuse: Syn. Erāng, Eger.

Gāmā—affixed to 'dā,' it means—'to rain.'

Gāmāng—to titillate.

Gāmbhir—grave.

Gāmchā—napkin; a short cloth.

Gan—umbra of the moon: so called because the moon is then said to be sitting with her courtiers, *e.g.*, Chandu-dubakiako, which means that the moon has an umbra.

Gaṇḍā—a set of four; one anna.

Gaṇḍe—oblique.

Gandhak—sulphur.

Gāndhi—a kind of insect emitting bad smell.

Gaṇḍu—a kind of small wooden chair.

Gan-gan—to turn round and round.

Gangā—the Ganges.

Gānjā—hemp.

Gānjāo—to heap up.

Gānjeri—one addicted to smoking gānjā.

Ganjhu—a big money-lender.

Gānji—cotton vest.

Gānṭi—to stir with a spoon while cooking: Syn. Ṭheo (*cf.* Beng. Ghonṭo).

Gāo—wound.

Gāonli—pertaining to a small village.

Gāonwār—indiscreet; foolish; a minor.

Gāoākān—wounded.

Gap sap—talk.

Gāpā—to-morrow.

Gāphlat }
Gāphlati } —negligence.

Gāpi—talkative.
Gara—ill luck (H., Beng., Gṛha).
Gārad'—jail.
Gāṛā—See Gāḍā.
Gārasāi-bongā—the deity who presides over childbirth.
Gaṛbar—confusion.
Gaṛ-baṛāo—to be confused.
Gardā—dust.
Gardān—to push by the neck.
Gāṛhā—a water channel.
Gāṛhā-loyong—a very low land.
Gāṛhā-goṛho—full of pits.
Garib—poor: Syn. Renge hoṛo.
Garjāo—to growl.
Garmi—syphilis.
Gaṛsar—average.
Gaṛur—any big bird.
Gasar—to cleanse utensils by rubbing.
Gāsij'—passing of winds.
Gati—relative; friend; companion; to clasp in arms; to go arm in arm (H.).
Gāṭi—limestone.
Gāṭi-gāṛā—a limestone quarry.
Gati-bāge—(*lit.* leaving the relations); the ceremony of formal demand of compensation from the bridegroom by the bride's female relations.
Gaudi—a distance of about 3 miles.
Ge—a form of addressing females; affixed to 'he' implying emphatic affirmation.
Gel, Geleā—ten.
Gemer—to seize and hold by the mouth.
Gena—edge; side: Syn. Atom, Jāpā.
Gendā—a ball.

Ger—to cut by the teeth as by a mouse or white ant.

Geṛe—a duck; a goose.

Ghāi—a spy; tale-bearer.

Ghamanḍi—to boast (H.).

Ghāni—oil press (H., Beng.).

Ghanṭā—bell; hour (H., Beng.).

Ghanṭi—a small bell (H., Beng.).

Ghāo—injury · wound (H., Beng.).

Ghar-dijoā—a son-in-law who is adopted in the family of the bride.

Ghaṛi—hour; time (H.).

Ghaṛi-kad'—a little while.

Ghāsi—a low-caste Hindu.

Ghaskāo—to escape; to slip away.

Ghāṭ—an elevated range.

Ghar-jo*n*reā—See Ghar dijoā.

Ghaṭal-bāṛhal—loss and profit.

Ghaṭāo—to shorten; to lose; to deduct; to fall short; to have an insufficient supply of (H.).

Ghāṭi—loss (H.).

Ghāṭwār—a watch-man on a ghāt.

Gheje-beje—filthy.

Ghināo—to hate.

Ghināo hoṛo—one who hates.

Gholāo—to get confused.

Ghornā—a hedge; a fence: Syn. Bakṛi.

Ghor-ghusiā—a lazy fellow; a stay at home.

Ghughurā—ankle bell.

Ghulghul—darkness caused by clouds.

Ghura*n*ṭ—circuitous: Syn. Biniur.

Ghurmuchāo—to twist: Syn. Penṭor.

Ghus—bribe.

Ghusā—to prod with fist.

Ghusāo—to cause to enter; to enter.

Giḍgiḍāo—to drag so as to make a rumbling sound.
Gij-gij'—filthy ; close together.
Gidi } —vulture.
Gidni }
Gini—a kind of small fish.
Gilā—moist (H.).
Gilṭi—swelling in the groin (H.).
Gilās—glass ; corrupt from of the English word 'glass.'
Gilipdār—to arrest.
Girā—a triangular fish net.
Giṛi—to throw away, to fall down ; used as a suffix denoting the doing of an act completely.
Girjā—church ; to join a religious service.
Girmiṭ—agreement made by the tea-garden coolies ; corrupt form of the word 'Agreement.'
Giru—red earth.
Giti—to lie down ; to sleep.
Gitioṛā—the sleeping room ; dormitory.
Gitil—sand ; insect.
Gitil ote—sandy soil.
Giu—shame ; modesty ; shyness.
Gojā—to sharpen to a point.
Gojākān—pointed.
Goālā—a Hindu caste ; those who tend cattle.
Goā } —witness ; to give evidence.
Gohā }
Gobar hoṭko—a kind of out-door game.
Gobrāha—dirty ; unclean.
Goe' } —to kill ; to die ; death.
Gojo }
God'—to pluck.
God'-aṛgu—to pluck and bring down.
Goḍā } —highland ; upland ; Syn. Piṛi, Tanṛ.
Goṛā }

Goḍā-bābā—upland paddy, which is harvested in August and September.

Godpaṛi—to go down on the head at one's feet.

Goeṭhā—dried cow-dung.

Go—to carry on the shoulder as in a Sikā-bāhingā.

Gogo—carrying on the shoulder.

Gohār—cow-shed : Syn. Uri-oṛā or Uri-gonṛā.

Gohār—to make a noise ; to raise a hue and cry.

Gol—circular ; round.

Gole'—to whistle.

Golā-māge-chānḍu—the month consisting of the second half of the Hindi month of Magh and the first half of the month of Phalgun.

Golmāl—noise ; confusion.

Gohom—wheat.

Gomke—sir ; master.

Go'nḍ—an aboriginal tribe of the Central Provinces.

Gondli—a kind of crop.

Gonong—price.

Gonong-ṭākā—bride price.

Gonong-toṛāoni—a negotiator of marriage; one who settles the bride price.

Goom—to winnow.

Gopoe'—reciprocal form of Goe'; to kill each other ; a deadly affray.

Gorā—fair : Syn. Esel.

Gossāin—a religious teacher.

Goso—to wither ; to anoint.

Goṭā—whole ; entire.

Gotā—to scratch the body to ease pains.

Goṭhāo—to round up cattle in order to lead them to a place of rest.

Goṭh—a place of rest for cattle.

Goṭhreko bongā—sacrificial ceremony to prevent cattle disease.

Gotong }
Gtom } —clarified butter; ghee.

Guchu—beard or moustache.

  Chetān-guchu—moustache.

  Lātār guchu—beard.

Gugulu—to cover the head, *e.g.*, with cloth.

Guiu—a shed for watching paddy.

Guḍu—a middle-sized rat.

Guji—a small room attached to a veranda.

Gulguliā—a wandering tribe.

Guli—shot ; a ball.

Gunā—fault; sin ; offence ; to commit an offence ; to offend.

Gunḍā—a pound ; pounded ; substance.

Gu*n*ḍi—a cow that is yoked to the plough.

Gunghi—a snail : Syn. Sooṭi.

Gungā—dumb : Syn. Gādi.

Gungu—elongated rain-hat made of leaves.

Gungu—father's elder brother : Syn. Baṛā.

Gu*n*j—the nail fixed to a top.

Gu*n*ṛ*n*i—saddle ; gunny cloth ; sack (H. Khogir).

Gupi—to graze cattle.

Gupini—one who tends cattle ; a cow-boy; a cow-herd.

Guṛ—molasses ; treacle.

Gurā—abcess.

Guṛākhu—tobacco.

Guṛguṛ—gravel : Syn. Rugud.

Guri—cow-dung.

Guṛlu }
Gu*n*dli } —a kind of crop (H. Gu*n*dli).

Guru—teacher ; sometimes used to denote a blacksmith, an artisan.

Gurul-gurul—to look with a fixed stare.

Guti—armpit.

Guṭu—a small jungle ; a small hillock ; used as a name-ending of villages, *e.g.*, Dāṛiguṭu.

H

Hā—expression used to drive away birds.

Hā-ā'-.—to be broken away by rush of water.

Hāb'—to bite.

Hābā—to fix; to entangle.

Hād'—to cut with knife.

Hāḍā—bullock (B. Dāngrā).

Hāḍād'—bitter (B. Hadhad).

Hāḍgāḍi—the ceremony of burying the bones of the dead: Syn. Jungtopa.

Hāḍhā—a hyena.

Hāḍi—expression used to drive away dogs.

Hāduṛ—to tumble down; to dismantle; to pull down.

Hāe—exclamation of sorrow.

Hāena—Alas.

Hāe-hāe—to lament.

Hāgā—brother.

Hāgā-hon.—nephew; brethren.

Hāgā-kimin—younger brother's wife.

Hāi—fish (B. Hāku; Sant. Hāko).

Different varieties of fishes: **Bālā hāi, Bing hāi, Budu hāi, Chirpi hāi, Choḍāhāi Ḍānḍikā hāi, Ichā hāi, Kātlā hāi, Linḍā hāi, Reḍā hāi, Ringir hāi, Rui hāi, Sunḍi-hāi.**

Hājām—a barber.

Hajam—to digest.

Hājat—imprisonment pending enquiry or trial.

Hājir—to be present.

Hājri—attendance.

Hajur—sir; Syn. Gomke.

Hak—right; claim; title.

Hākā—to hang up; to suspend (B.).

Hākā-bākā / Ākā-bākā—to be surprised; to wonder; to be taken aback: Syn. Aka-danda (B.).

Hālā / Hāllā—noise; uproar.

Hālāng—to pick up; to collect by picking (B.),

Halap—oath; solemn affirmation: Syn. Kiriā-jom.

Halbāl—restless.

Hālchāl—news.

Hālkā—light; an instrument for levelling earth.

Halumān—black-faced monkey.

Halwai—sweetmeat vendor.

Hāmāl / Hāmbāl—weighty; heavy; difficult; impossible; pregnant [(B.).

Hāmbāl-bābā—lowland paddy ripening late in the season.

Hāmbāl-kāṭā—*lit.* heavy foot; pregnancy.

Hān—yonder; at a distance; there (Sant. Hande).

Hānā—yonder one; yonder ones (inanimate).

Hānāb-gonoe—epilepsy.

Hānār—mother-in-law (B. Hānhār).

Hānāṭing—noun form of Hāṭing; division; share; a part.

Hānāko—those over there (inanimate).

Hānḍā—a big earthen pot.

Hā*n*ḍed'—to shut up (B. ha*n*ṛed')

Hā*n*ḍiā—country liquor.

Hāndiṛio—to fall; to collapse (as a wall); to tumble down.

Hā*n*ḍne—afternoon; 2 to 3 P.M.: Syn. Tar-singi.

Hānḍsā—to beat; to whip.

Hanḍu—mosquitoes (B. Bhusṛi).

Hāngāmā—a riot or affray.

Hāngi—a large ditch: Syn. Huāng.

Hāni—yonder one (animate).

Hān-king—the two over there or yonder (animate).

Hān-ko—those yonder (animate).

Hān-terā
Hān-rā } —of that (yonder) place.

Hānsā—that side; that way.

Hā*n*sā—a swan.

Hān-te
Hāntāre } —there; at a distance; yonder.

Hān te nete—here and there; hither and thither (Sant. Onte note).

Hāo-mui—a large red ant.

Hap'
Hab' } —to bite.

Hāpād'—leeches.

Hāpārub-joār—to salute each other.

Hāpāṭing—to divide among each other; reciprocal form of Hāṭing.

Hāpe—to keep quiet (B.).

Hāpe-hāpe—slowly; by and by.

Haptā—week.

Hāpu—a bat.

Hān—to drive; to drive away; to wear out.

Hāṛā—ox; bullock (B. Dangṛā).

Hārā—to grow up: Syn. Omon (B.).

Hār-uṛung
Hār-oḍong } —to drive out; to drive away.

Hāṛād'—bitter; pungent (B. Hāṛhād).

Hāṛām—old; to become old (B.).

Hāṭār—to hang a child on the back by wrapping it up with cloth.

Hārāo—to defeat.

Hāṛāpāṭā—to get knotted (*cf.* Beng. Jaṛāpaṭki).

Hārdāng—a kind of outdoor game.

Hāṛgāṛi
Hāṛ-sāṛi } —burial ground.

Hāṛi—expression used to drive away dogs.

Hāriār—green.

Harkā—a bamboo basket with lids.

Hārob—to become well ; to be cured ; to be convalescent.

Hartā—bark of a tree (Sant., B.).

Hārub—to cover ; to shut or close up an umbrella.

Hār-wāhā—ploughman : Syn. Siuni.

Hāsā—earth ; mud ; soil (Sant. Has).

Hāsi—fun.

Hāsli—necklet of metal.

Hāsu—illness ; to be ill ; to suffer (Beng. Asukh).

Hāsulij-āng }
Hāsṛi-jāng } —the collar-bone

Hāsur—See Āsur.

Hāsur—to set ; to go down ; setting of the sun or moon.

Hāsuṛu—to cease raining.

Hāṭ—bazar ; market : Syn. Peeṭ.

Hātā—compound.

Hātāng—brain (B.).

Hāṭāo—to cause to recede ; to separate.

Hātāoṛi—hammer.

Hātnā—a kind of timber tree (H. Arjun).

Hāt-hiār—an instrument; a weapon.

Hāth-kaṛi—handcuff.

Hāṭi kuṭi—miscellaneous ; of various kinds.

Hāṭing—to divide ; to partition.

Hāṭing-ni—one who divides.

Hātoāl—bow-string.

Hātom—father's sister (B.).

Hātu—village (Sant. Āto).

Hātu ete }
Hātu āte } —from the village.

Hātu jāpā-piṛi—lands on the outskirts of a village basti.

Hātu bongā—deity presiding over the village.

Hātu-disum—*lit.* the country of the village ; native country.

Hātu ren }
Hātu rā } —belonging to the village ; of the village.

Hāyā—desire ; lust ; passion.

He—yes ; to assent ; to agree ; true.

He }
Hai } —relative interjection, used to draw one's attention.
Āteā }

He-derāng—of course.

He ge—that's true ; agreed ; yes ; of course.

He-kedā—*lit.*—said 'Yes' ; admitted ; agreed.

He mār—yes ; very well.

He-mār }
He-oṛo } —that's plain enough or quite clear ; oh, yes.

He mār bes }
He to be } —very well ; all right then.

He-to—yes ; very well.

Hebe—to take up a child in arms or lap.

Hebe-jom—to bear a child ; to give birth to a child.

Heben—astringent taste (B. Kasā).

Hej'—to pluck leaves from tree (B.).

Helā—oh ! hallo ! an expression calling one's attention.

Helā }
Oh-re } —exclamations of astonishment and surprise.

Helāo }
Hilāo } —to move ; to shake.

Helmel—friendly.

Hemrom—a Munda sept.

Hen—strong form of 'en' used to express contempt or hatred.

Hende—black.

Hendo—to echo back ; to mock ; to ridicule.

Hengān—to rub against something; to sharpen; to polish.
Henṛem—sweet: Syn. Sibil (B.).
Hen-tāre—that; side.
Hente—same as Hānte.
Hente nete—here and there.
Hepājat—custody; to take care of.
Her—to sow (B.).
Heṛā—late; delay; to delay (B. Bera).
Herā—to visit occasionally (B. Lel-agu).
Heṛān—near by; in front of.
Heṛe—chaff; husk of rice (B.).
Herea—anything to be sown.
Heṛed'—to weed by the hand; final weeding; weed (B.).
Her jeṭeā—dry sowing: *lit.* sowing in summer.
Herel—full-grown man; husband (B.).
Heṛem—See Henṛem.
Her pher—topsy-turvy.
Hesā—a kind of tree (H. Pipar).
Hesel / **Hesel dāru**—a kind of tree (H. Ḍha-oṭhā).
Hetā—to look behind.
Hetā-bāṛā—to look around (B. Lel-bāṛā).
Heṭā-ruāṛ—to look back again.
Hewā—to accustom; to get accustomed; to be familiar.
Hiā—to his cough.
Hiām-hiām—to speak in whispers.
Hiāting—to feel affection for; to feel pity.
Hichir—the flash of lightning; to flash.
Higāṛ—to round up one's own cattle and separate (B.).
Hiju—to come; used as an adjective to signify something coming.
Hiju ākān—arrived; present.
Hiju me—come! come here.
Hiju-nām—to come in search of.

Hiju-ni—one who comes.

Hiju senotān—coming and going ; to frequent.

Hilā—to hate ; to neglect (B., Beng. Helā).

Hilāng—to feel a repulsion ; a feeling of repulsion.

Hilāo—See Helao.

Hili } —elder brother's wife (B.).
Hilim }

Hing—asafoetida.

Hinsāti—to despise, to envy.

Hir—to fan (B. Dhu*n*kāo).

Hirā—diamond.

Hiṛā-ā—to hiccough : Syn. Hiā.

Hirā-āu—to come back after visiting somebody.

Hirchi—to sprinkle (B.).

Hiriti } —love ; affection ; concord ; cordiality (*cf.* Sans. Prīti).
Pirti }

Hisi—twenty ; score (B., Sant. Isi ; Beng., H. Bis).

Hisingā—to hate ; envy.

Hisir—bead ; necklace (B.).

Hitā—seed (B., H. Bihin).

Hobā—to be ; to become (B., Beng. Hae).

Hobā jānā—has become or has been done.

Hobā jānre—if that be so ; that being done.

Hobāoā—will be ; will happen : used with other verbs to form the future time (Beng. Hoibe).

Hobā-ote—fertile land.

Hod'—to tear and break up.

Hokā—to stop ; to end ; to put a stop to (B.).

Holā—yesterday (B., Beng. Kāl).

Holā-tere—the day before yesterday.

Holād—razor (B.).

Hole—to take off ; to put off (B.).

Holong—flour ; bread : Syn. Lad' (B.).

Hon—son ; child ; the young one (B.) : used with other nouns to indicate the diminitive sense.

Hon bā parab—a festival celebrated in the month of Baisaka or Jet (May-June) just before sowing is done in the village.

Hon-ḍāṛo—the little finger.

Honā kiā—to give birth (to a child).

Honā kimin—son's wife (B.).

Honāng—perhaps ; may be ; indicates probability or possibility.

Honāngā—used as a suffix to the conditional form to indicate desire, *e. g.*, 'I wish I could.'

Honḍā—to stir while cooking.

Hondej'—to boil with a sound (B.).

Honder—that.

Honder-honder—used as an adjective to signify some previous date, *e.g.*, honder-honder chanḍu.

Honder }
Honder-hulāng }—day before yesterday.

Hon-gaṅṛā—children ; issue.

Hon-hopon—children ; descendants.

Honjār—father-in-law (B.).

Hon-kāṭu—smaller toes.

Hon-kiā—same as Honā kiā.

Hon-ko—sons ; future generations.

Honor—to wander or walk here and there.

Hon-tāio-kuchu—womb.

Hon-te-koṛā—son.

Hooni—a big rat.

Hopon—an insect which drills through wood (Beng. Ghun).

Hopor—near : Syn. Jāpā (B. Gena).

Hopor-jāpā—round about.

Horā—road ; path (B.).

Horāte—by the way ; through ; with the help of.

Hoṛe—a kind of pulse ; *Dolichus biflorus* (H. Kurthi, B.).

Hoṛmo—physical body (B.).

Horo—to keep watch.

Hoṛo—man ; a Munda as opposed to foreigners.

Hoṛo-kāji—*lit.* the language of man, meaning the Muḍāsi language.

Horo—tortoise ; a Munḍā sept (B.).

Hoṛo honko—the sons of man ; mankind in general, meaning the Munḍā race.

Hoṛo-hoṛo—man by man ; each man.

Horoni } —watchman ; guard.
Ogrā }

Horsod'—to thrust ; to insert (B.).

Hos—sense ; consciousness.

Hosongor—to slip off.

Hosoṛo } —falsehood ; a lie ; false (Sant. Nase).
Hosoṛ }

Hoṭā—to attack with horns erect : Syn. uṭub', to prick., as with a needle.

Hoṭo—neck ; the throat.

Hoṭor—to thrust ; to prod (B., H. Hurā).

Hoyo—air ; wind (B., Beng., H. Haoa).

Hoyo—to shave (B.).

Hoytāni—barber.

Huā—to bite ; to snap.

Huāng—a ditch ; a pit ; a deep drain.

Huāṛā—the green pigeon.

Hubāng giṛi—to cast away after cutting.

Hudiṛ—to cut slightly ; bruise.

Huḍumā—to throw ; to hurl ; to cast away (B. Lebda).

Huḍuṛing—a few ; a little.

Huḍuṛing lekā—in small quantities.

Hujat—oppress ; to annoy.

Hujul—*lit.* to shake the body ; to trot ; to walk fast with loads on both sides of a bāhāngi.

Hujur—sir : Syn. Gomke.

Hukum—order ; decision.

Hukur—a low moan or growl ; the cry of a buffalo.

Hul—to vomit : Syn. Ulā.

Hulā—to break into pieces (B. Huchā).

Hulāng—day (B., H. Roj) : Syn. Dilāng.

Huliā—hue and cry.

Humā—to beat : Syn. Dāl (B. Piṭāo, Rui).

Humu—filth ; dirt ; dirty (B.).

Hunḍi—to collect ; to gather together (B.).

Hunḍi-ākān—collected or brought together ; assembled.

Hupuā—reciprocal form of Huā ; to bite each other.

Hupuṛing—very little ; very few.

Hur—swan.

Hurāng—a sling ; to throw as from a sling.

Huṛār—hyena.

Hu-ri—a kind of plant (H. Sinduār ; Beng. Nishiudā).

Huṛing—a little ; small ; a few (B.).

Huṛing ḍāḍo—the middle finger ; the ring finger.

Huṛing ge—dear ; high-priced.

Huṛing-huṛing—small ; in small quantities.

Huṛing-jiu—to be disappointed.

Huṛing-lekā—some ; few ; a little.

Huṛing-ni—the younger one.

Huṛing-utar—the smallest.

Huṛkā—wooden bar for a door.

Hurum Suku } —honey (B. Horomsi) of the Hurum Suku bee.
Hurum Suku Rasi }

Hurum Suku Engā—a species of small honey bee.

Hurum Suku Dā—the bee-hive of the Hurum Suku bee.

Hụsiār—intelligent ; alert (H.)

Husid'—to scrape off or cut off the surface : Syn. Lā (B. Ged).

Huṭā—to break.

Huṭir—to snore (B. Huṭkir).

Huṭub—a large stone slab ; a small hillock.

I

I—expression of surprise.

I—suffix, to form definite demonstrative pronouns from definite demonstrative adjectives, *e. g.*, Hijutan-i—the one who comes, hijulen-i—the one who came ; senken-i—the one who went.

Iām—to weep ; to cry ; to grieve (B.).

Ibil—dense ; density ; thick ; close together ; condensed; concentrated.

Ichā—to pinch (B.).

Ichā-bā—a kind of flower (B. Dhawaiba).

Ichā-hāi—prawn ; a kind of fish (B., Sant. Ichā haku).

Ichi / Iri—to let ; to permit : used as a suffix to other verbs, *e. g.*, Sen-ichi, to let (one) go.

Idāng—early ; morning (B. Angur).

Idi—to take (B., Sant.).

Idime—take.

Idu—possibly, gives the idea of uncertainty, implying 'I don't know.'

Idu-dāng / Idu-tām—perhaps ; may be.

Idu-oṛo—who knows ? perhaps.

Ih'—an exclamation of surprise.

Ij'—stool ; to pass stools.

Ijāhār—deposition ; to depose.

Ij'-poṭom—one who always passes stools ; a term of abuse.

Ijārā—lease.

Ijārdār—lessee.

Ikir—deep; depth (B. Gahir).
Ikir-bongā—the spirit of a deep pool.
Ikṛi-sikṛi—noisy; mischievous; restless (Sant. Ekel-sekel).
Ikṛum—to kneel (B. Ikṛum).
Il—feather.
Ilākā—country; jurisdiction.
Ilām-baksis—reward.
Ili—rice-beer: Syn. Boḍej' (B.).
Iling—to throng round and push: Syn. Uduṛ (B.).
Ili-rānu—fermenting medicine (roots of certain trees) (B.).
Im
Ihim } —liver (B.).
Imān—truth; honesty (H.).
Imāndār—honest; truthful (H.).
Imin
Āmin } —this; like this; that much; so much (animate).
Imināng—that much; so much; just so many (inanimate).
Imināng ge—that much only (Sant. Ināg).
Imin-reo—yet; notwithstanding; still.
Imtā
Imtā-ge } —then; at once; immediately.
Imtāng—that time; then (B. Imis or Imitā).
Imtihān—examination.
In—a variant of the suffix 'en.'
Ināte
Enāte
Enāmente } —therefore; for that reason (Sant.).
Inchi—inch.
Indārā—well.
Ind chānḍu—the Mundari month calculated from the new moon day in the Hindi month of Bhado.
Ind parab—a festival celebrated on the 11th day after the new moon in the month of Bhado, also called 'Karam.'

Ing }
Āing } —I.

Ing-āte—from me; by me.

Ing-tā—with me; in my possession.

Ingtāte—from me; from my place.

Ing-tā-re—with me; in my place.

Ini—he; this one (animate). (Sant., B. Muni; Beng. Ini, Tini)

Iniā—his.

Inichi—is it he?

Ini-ete—from him; by him.

Inirā }
Iniā } —his.

Ini-tāre—to him; of him; from him.

In-king—these two; they (two) (animate).

In ku—they (more than two) (animate).

In kuā—their; of those.

Inṛi—to put out (fire); to go out (fire); a game; a variant of 'Enṛe.'

Inṭā—brick.

Inung—to play (B. Ene).

Ipāege—empty-handed.

Ipidi—reciprocal form of Idi.

Ipil—star; pupil of the eye.

Ipil ārā—a kind of vegetable, sour in taste (H. Kudrum).

Ipiṛi piung—glow-worm (B. Bhagjogni).

Ir—to reap; to cut any crop (Sant.).

Irālia }
Iriliā } —eight.

Iril koṛā—husband's younger brother (B. Priul).

Iril kuṛi—husband's younger sister (B.).

Iril-sā—eight times.

Irirlia—eight each.

Irkhāo—to hate; to be jealous or spiteful.

Iro—harvest.
Iro-ko—those who harvest or cut crops.
Isā—Jesus Christ.
Isāi—Christian.
Isiāṛā—bile bag.
Isin—to boil ; to cook rice or any hard eatable (B.).
Isināknā—boiled.
Ising—to-day : Syn. Tising (B. Tihing).
Iskul—school.
Isor—God.
Ispāt—steel.
Istihār—notice ; proclamation.
Istāphā—surrender ; resignation.
Istok—up to ; all.
Isu—many ; much ; great.
Isu purā—very much ; very many ; very great.
Iswi—Christian era.
Iṭā—brick.
Itihās—history ; story.
Iṭkid—to rub with the hand.
Iṭil—fat (B. Chaki).
Iṭir—to rub ; to massage (B.).
Itu—to teach ; teacher ; to preach.
Ituān—knowing ; one who knows.
Ituānā—to know.
Itun—to learn.
Ituni—teacher.
Itun tāni—one who learns ; student.

J

Jā—used as a suffix to mean 'perhaps,' 'may be.
Jā—any at all ; some (animate).
Jā-e—any (singular).

Jā-ege—any one ; any one at all.

Jā-ege
Jā-hoṛo } —any man.

Jā-hulāng—any day ; ever.

Jā-imtāng—at any time.

Jāimināng—any amount of ; any number of.

Jā-iminreo—although.

Jā-king—any two.

Jā-ko—any ones at all.

Jāe ko
Jānko } —any (plural).

Jā-lekāte—anyhow ; by any means.

Jā-n—some ; any (inanimate).

Jā-nā—any (inanimate).

Jānā-jetānā
Jānā-ge } —anything at all.

Jā-ni—any (animate).

Jān-king—any two.

Jān-ko—any one.

Jā-rege—anywhere ; everywhere (B.)

Jabāb—reply ; written statement.

Jābur—force.

Jabhā—to cut.

Jābid'
Jābit' } —to attach.

Jabrāi—forcibly.

Jad'—much more ; great many.

Jādu—magic ; spell ; charm.

˙—simple present tense suffix (transitive).

tāikena—indefinite present imperfect suffix (transitive).

ır—a kind of song, sung during the Bā-Parab or a little before that (Sant.).

ɡir—grant of land.

jāt—property.

Jāe-jug—always; for ever.
Jāe-julum—to insist greatly.
Jāgāh—place.
Jāgāo—to awaken.
Jagar—to talk ; to tell ; to speak.
Jāgran—the day preceding a festival.
Jāhāj—ship.
Jahar—poison : Syn. Bisi, Mohurā.
Jāher } —sacred grove or sarnā.
Jāiār }
Jāher sarnā—sacred grove.
Jāin koṛā—son's or daughter's son (B.).
Jāin kuṛi—son's or daughter's daughter (B.).
Jāir—same as Jāher.
Jājak—priest (*cf.* Sans. Yājaka).
Jāked—till ; until.
Jakham—wound : Syn. Ghao.
Jāl—net ; to lick.
Jālāting—to fly or hover about (B.).
Jalbhātā—tomato (B. Belāti).
Jāli—blind ; cataract of the eye : Syn. Dundu (B. Jala).
Jāliā—a forgerer ; a cheat.
Jaljalāo—to clean to brightness.
Jalkhari—a net to suspend something.
Jālom—a fishing net ; a temporary shed to accommodate the bridegroom's party in the house of the bride ; to entrap (Sant., *cf.* Sans. Jāla).
Jamā—to gather together ; total.
Jamādār—a constable.
Jāmḍā } —a pandal of leaves.
Jāmbṛā }
Jāmin—bail ; surety.
Jāmindār—surety ; bailor.
Jān—incomplete past tense or pluperfect suffix.

Jānā—indefinite past tense suffix.
Janam—birth ; to be born.
Janamjug—for ever ; always.
Jānāo—at any time ; always ; ever.
Jānās-jānāo—for ever ; from generation to generation.
Jā*n*ch—to enquire ; to substantiate ; enquire : Syn. Kuli-uṛung (*lit.* to bring out by asking).
Janeu—sacred thread.
Jāng—bone ; bone of the upper part of the leg ; seed of any grain.
Jangan-jo—a fruit with seed.
Jāngbāhā } **Jāng-topā** }—the ceremony of burial of the bones of the dead.
Jān-jetān—anything ; any place, etc.
Jānjid—bamboo net : Syn. Kumni.
Jānoā-hon—twin children (Beng. Jamaj).
Jāntā-diri—grinding-stone.
Jānum—thorn ; thorny plant.
Jānwār—animal.
Jao—barley.
Jāpā—near ; side ; edge (B. Henad).
Japagar—reciprocal form of Jagar.
Jāpāre—in the vicinity.
Jāpi—the name given to a kind of dance or song—usually sung at the spring season.
Jāpid—blindfold ; to close the eyes (B.).
Jārā—castor plant ; *Palma christi* (H. Erendi).
Jārgi—rains (B.).
Jārgi-dā—rainy season.
Jāri—to promulgate an order.
Jaribānā } **Jurbānā** }—fine.
Jaṛibuṭi—medicinal herbs and roots.
Jārom—egg ; to ripen ; ripe.

Jarur—certainly.

Jāsti—much : Syn. Timbā, Purā.

Jāṭā—twigs used as fuel.

Jāti }
Jāt } —caste.

Jāt-pāt—castes and customs.

Jatan—to nurse ; to care.

Jātrā—festival ; fair.

Je—a variant of Jā.

Jehel—to imprison : Syn. Tol.

Jehel Khānā—jail.

Je-lekā—of some sort ; any sort.

Jembed'—to suck (B. Chopor).

Jenget'—bright and sparkling.

Jer }
Jeir } —root.

Jere—fluid exuding from a tree when cut.

Jered'—to paste together.

Jerkā—twin, *e. g.*, twin fruits, twin fingers, etc.

Jeṭ—the month of Jeth ; eldest.

Jetā—some ; any (inanimate).

Jetāe—any one ; some one (animate).

Jetāeo—even any.

Jetān—some ; any (inanimate).

Jetānā—any ; anything (inanimate).

Jetāni—anyone ; some one (animate).

Jetān king—some two.

Jetān ko—some ones.

Jetā-sāre—some where.

Jeṭe—hot ; heat : Syn. Balbal (B. Udgar, Situng).

Jeṭer—to dry anything over a fire : Syn. Tersāng, Roṛ (B.).

Jeṭe sā }
Jeṭe singi } —hot season ; summer.

Jeṭ sārā—wife's elder brother.

Jhālā pulā—gaudy dress.

Jhāli—net.

Jhalkāo— to flash ; to burn.

Jhakmakāo—to shine ; to flash.

Jhānḍā—pole with a flag attached to it.

Jhānjrā—sieve.

Jhā*n*ṭ—hairs on the private parts.

Jhāp—to hurl oneself into : Syn. Satintānā.

Jhapṭāo—to swoop down to catch.

Jhārā—seasoned wood.

Jhāṛiā—shower of rain.

Jhingā—cucumber.

Jholā—cloth bag.

Jhompā—a cluster or bunch.

Jhumur—a kind of song sung in Tamar area.

Jhunḍ—bunch ; a thick gathering.

Jhupṛi—a small straw hut.

Jhuri—twigs.

Jhuṭiā—toe ring.

Jhuṭhā—false.

Jhuṭ phus—false.

Ji—to smell (B.).

Ji-bodeme—have patience.

Jiān—to die ; death.

Jiāng—grandmother (Sant. Jiā ; B. Āji).

Jiāo—to preserve alive.

Jid'—to come to life ; to revive ; to live (B. Jiad).

Ji }
Jiu } —life.

Ji }
Jidhā } —to be obstinate ; to make a determination.

Ji-ghātan—perverse ; *lit.* one who kills the soul.

Jiki—porcupine (B. Jik).

Ji'-lā—patience.
Jilā—district.
Jilād'—to slip ; slippery.
Jiling—long; length; far ; to stretch out (Sant. Jelen; B.).
Jilu—meat ; flash ; deer ; games.
Jimā—charge ; custody ; to give in charge of ; to entrust ; control; possession.
Jinis—thing ; article ; property.
Jingā—a kind of vegetable (H. Jhingā).
Jinṛi—hemp.
Jio, Jiā—blessing ; to bless.
Jipling—long.
Jir—to fan.
Jirki—quicksand.
Jirub', Jurup'—to warm oneself by fire (B.).
Jisu—Jesus.
Jitāo—to win.
Jiu—life.
Jin-jatan—great eare.
Jiu-oṛā—uterus ; vagina.
Jo—fruit ; to bear fruit (Sant., B.).
Jo-sā—time to fruit.
Jo', Jono—broom-stick.
Joā—cheek (B. Johā).
Joāo—to cause to grow ; to allow to grow.
Joār, Johār—to salute.
Joārni—one who welcomes the guests (bridegroom's party) on the occasion of a marriage ceremony.
Jobān—word ; promise.
Jobhi—swampy ground.

Jobod′ }
Jābid′ } —to attach.

Jod′—to wipe off and dry.

Jogāo—to keep carefully ; to save.

Jogāo—to nurse.

Johār—salutation ; praise ; to salute ; to hail (B.).

Jojo—sour ; acid ; tamarind (Sant., B.).

Jojom—eating for the purpose of eating.

Jok }
Jokā } —to measure ; to compare (Sant.).
Jujāo }

Jokā—equal ; to aim (B. Jokhā).

Jolhā—a Musalman weaver (Sant.).

Jolom—to plaster, *e. g.*, a wall or floor.

Jom—to eat ; used as a suffix, meaning, for oneself, *e. g.*, Āu-jom, to bring for oneself (Sant., B.).

Jomeā—food ; a feast.

Jom ichi }
Jom-rikā } —to feed : Syn. Ajom (B. Ajom).

Jom-hoṛoko }
Jojom-hoṛoko } —the people who will eat.

Jom nāwā—the ceremony of eating new rice ; there is no fixed time.

Jom Rājā—God of death.

Jom rikā—to feed.

Jom-sā—right side.

Jom-teā—food.

Jomti—right hand (Sant., B.).

Joṇḍrā—maize (Sant., B. Janra).

Jono—a sweeping brush ; broom (B.).

Jono ipil—comet.

Jonokā—parable ; example.

Jontor—a child of ten or eleven years (male or female).

Jopoār—reciprocal form of Joā.

Jo'—to sweep (B. Joh').

Jo'-āming—to dust off or cleanse by sweeping (B.).

Jor—force : Syn. Peṛe.

Joṛā—a pair.

Joro—to ooze out ; to issue ; to trickle ; to leak out (B.).

Joroipoṭā—a poor hungry man (B. Jorpoṭa).

Joti—The rope by which animals are yoked.

Jovi—marshy land.

Ju—exhortative particle signifying 'go.'

Ju-senome—good-bye then.

Juā—gambling.

Ju-ulā }
Julā } —kitchen ; hearth (H. Chulhā).

Judā—to separate ; different.

Jug—age ; ancient time.

Jugi—weavers of woollen blankets.

Jugut'—circumspection.

Jul'—to kindle ; to burn) .).

Jumbā—a bower.

Jumbṛi }
Jumbuṛi } —covetous ; gluttonous (B. Jumri).

Jumlā—gather ; total ; a collection.

Jumpā—a cluster ; a bunch.

Jundi—to kindle.

Junkā—hanging.

Junkājilu—calf of the leg.

Junul—flame ; brightness ; glory.

Jupuṭid—to touch each other.

Juṛā—to join ; to stick.

Juṛi—a pair ; match ; equal (B. Jori).

Juru—to surround ; to throng round.

Jurup'—to warm oneself by the fireside.

Juṭhā—leavings of one's food.

Juṭi—to seduce (B. Puslao).

Juṭid—to join together ; to touch (B. Joted).

K

Kā—(1) no : indicates negative sense.
(2) shortened form of lekā—used as a suffix.
(3) affixed to certain verbs to denote imperative mood, *i.e.*, inku hiju kā ko—let them come.
(4) in order that.

Kā
Kākā } —paternal uncle (H., Beng.).

Kā-āni—story ; folk-tale.

Kā-ge—no.

Kā-gedo—certainly not.

Kā-redo—otherwise ; or else (B. Bāngredo).

Kābāng-kubung—said of one walking in a stooping posture (*i.e.*, so weak that the spine is bent).

Kābār
Chitar kābār } —spotted, specially red and white.

Kābil—fit ; capable : Syn. Dāṛilekā.

Kabjā—possession ; control : Syn. Ti ; Aktiār.

Kābrā
Kābri } —*vide* Kābār.

Kābu—invalid ; tired.

Kābuā—*lit.* not our, *i. e.*, we won't.

Kabul—to agree ; to admit ; to acknowledge.

Kābuli—an Afghan.

Kabuliat—counterpart of a lease.

Kāch—glass : Syn. Āenā.

Kā-chi—isn't it ?

Kāchā—unripe : Syn. Berel, Peṭo.

Kāchā—pice : Syn. Paisā, Ḍibuā.

Kāchhāri—court.

Kach-kach—to tease.
Kach-pach—restless.
Kāchrā } —sapwood : Syn. Jāṭājuri.
Kāchri }
Kachuā—tortoise ; a Munda sept.
Kāḍā } —buffalo.
Keḍā }
Kadal—plantain (Sans. Kadalī).
Kadal Dāru—plantain-tree.
Kadam—trot.
Kadam Dāru—a kind of tree ; *Anthocephalus Kadamba*.
Kadar—kind ; method ; manner.
Kadrāo—to be discontented ; offended (Sant.).
Kaḍṛu—a young male buffalo.
Kaduā—pumpkin : Syn. Suku.
Kaed—imprisonment.
Kaedi—convict ; prisoner.
Kāgaj—paper.
Kai Kai—to whine, as a jackal.
Kāi*n*ā—I won't.
Kāi*n*ti } —knife used in a cock-fight (B.).
Kāit }
Kahā-Kahi—to discuss angrily : Syn. Japagar, Kāpāji.
Kāhāni } —tale ; story ; saying.
Kā-āni }
Kāhār —a Hindu caste.
Kāhele—why : Syn. Chināmente.
Kā-khānḍā—a kind of fish.
Kājar—eye-paint.
Kāji—to speak ; to say ; to tell ; a talk ; news (B. Gām).
Kājibāṛā—to tell about ; to spread a rumour.
Kājibeṛā—to publish.
Kāji idi āgu—messenger of a 'Pārhā' panch.
Kāji-jān—promised ; foretold

Kāji-Kāniāh—folk-tales.

Kāji-ruāṛ—to reply.

Kāji-runuār—answer.

Kāji-seterni—*lit.* reacher of the word ; angel.

Kājirā-Jukutu—a proverb.

Kājirā-dāsiko—*lit.* servants of the Word ; preachers.

Kākā—father's younger brother.

Kākā—to caw (crows).

Kākā Gungu—*lit.* father's younger brother and father's elder brother : used to signify the relationship between their sons.

Kā kānā—brass bracelet : Syn. Sākom (Sans. Kaṅkaṇa).

Kāki, Kāki engā—father's younger brother's wife.

Kāklā—to talk ; converse ; to call loudly ; to make a noise ; talkative.

Kākṛu—sweet pumpkin.

Kal—a machine.

Kālā—deaf (B. Bahira).

Kālāpāni—an island ; signifies the Andamans.

Kal kalāo—to make a noise.

Kālom—next year ; ensuing year (Sant., B.).

Ne Kālom—this year.

Kalu—oil-press.

Kālu—a leaf-cup.

Kām—not you.

Kāmāi—earning.

Kamal—lotus : a Munda sept in Tamar Pergana.

Kāmān—shaving, as a ceremoney of purification after death, in a family.

Kāmi—to work ; work.

Kāmiā—a labourer.

Kāmi-hoṛo—one who works hard.

Kāmrā } —woollen blanket.
Kām ṛ ṇā }

Kām ṛi—maid-servant.

Kānābāsi—yoke hook.

Kānātab—fasting.

Kanausi—a small ear-ring.

Kanbāuri—a long ear-ring.

Kānchi } —a wide-mouthed bamboo basket.
Khānchi }

Kāndhā—a sort of fine imposed on an outcaste to readmit him into caste.

Kandhar—cave.

Kānḍom—brink or edge of a vessel (B. Kana; Beng. Kānā).

Kāneā ḍāḍo—the little finger : Syn. Hon-ḍaḍo.

Kāni sārsār—nail of the little finger : loosely used for the little finger.

Kānistibil—constable.

Kānji—a preparation of rice-water.

Kānjgi—a week old rice-water.

Kānju—to fall into a pit.

Kankan—very cold : Syn. Tutkun.

Kānki—to look with one eye closed.

Kānpāti—temple of the head.

Kā*n*ṛā—ophthalmia.

Kānṭā—weighing scale.

Kānṭāṛā—jack fruit.

Kānṭāṛā inung—a kind of outdoor game.

Kāpā—to throw into the mouth (B. Topa).

Kāpāji—reciprocal form of Kāji ; talk ; discussion ; quarrel ; altercation ; wrangle (B. Gapam : *cf.* Beng. Kājiā—riot).

Kāpi—a kind of axe (Sant.).

Kapti—deceitful ; dishonest ; insincere.

Kapur—camphor.

Kar—rent.

Kārā }
Kārhā } —earth remover, used in levelling earth; to level the earth.

Kaṛāhi—a frying pan.

Karaili—a kind of vegetable.

Karam—a kind of tree, held sacred by the Mundas (*Nauclea parvifolia*).

Karam ḍāir—a sworn friend.

Karam—a festival celebrated on the 11th day after the new moon in the month of Bhādo.

Karanchā—a fox: Syn. Tuyu (B. Tuyu).

Karanjo—a kind of tree, the seed of which is pressed for oil (*Pongamia glabra*).

Karār—to promise; agreement.

Karaṭ—thread-twister; bobbin.

Kaṛbā—handle of a plough.

Kārbār—trade; business.

Kārbāria—agent.

Kārchhul—iron ladle.

Kārdhāni }
Khārdāni } —a sort of belt worn round the waist.

Kāṛhā—a sort of instrument for levelling earth. Big ones are called Ataṛgom.

Karheni—a kind of paddy.

Kāṛe—oil cake (B. Kalka; H. Khari; Beng. Khail).

Kāre hisir—bead made of *kasi* grass stalks.

Kāre—a kind of grass (H. Kasi).

Karetal—cymbal.

Kā-redo—but if not; or else; otherwise (B. Bang redo).

Kā redo kā—or else; not at all.

Kārigar—a trained man.

Kāṛihon—a young she-buffalo.

Kāril—bamboo shoots: Syn. Helta, Hānḍuā-utu.

Karjā—debt : Syn. Rinṛi.

Karkad'—twigs used as tooth brush.

Kaṛkaṛāo—to heat any liquid.

Kārkhānā—workshop.

Kāṛ kom / **Kāṭ kom**—crab (Sans. Karkaṭa ; Beng. Kåkṛā).

Kārpā / **Khārpā**—a sort of leather sandal or slippers (B. Khārpa).

Karrā—very stiff.

Kartāl / **Karetāl**—cymbal (B., Beng. Karatāl).

Kaṛor—a kind of bird.

Kaṛuā—hot : pungent; Syn. Hāṛād'.

Kasā—astringent : Syn. Heben (Sans. Kasāya).

Kasāi—butcher.

Kasam—oath : Syn. Kiriā.

Kasāo—to tighten : Syn. Keṭe.

Kāsom—cotton (Sans. Kārpāsa ; Beng. Kāpās ; H. Rui).

Kasaṭ—pains : Syn. Duku.

Kāsi—a kind of grass : Syn. Kāre.

Kāsmār—a species of fruit tree.

Kasrā—itches : Syn. Pusri.

Kasur—fault; sin; guilt ; offence; to commit an offence.

Kāṭ—a measure of grain, about 30 to 40 seers ; a measure of land having a seed area of 30 to 40 seers : Syn. Sālā.

Kāṭā—leg; foot (Sant., B.).

Kāṭā-ābungni—feet-washer of guests.

Kāṭā jāmbāṛā / **Kāṭā jāmā sā**—south.

Kāṭā tālkā—sole of the foot.

Kāṭā-topānā—a form of trial by ordeal in deciding boundary disputes.

Kātāb'—fasting; to fast (B. Upas).

Kāṭāo—to strike out.

Kāṭe—when suffixed to 'gama' it means, to continue raining.

Kāṭeā—a mouse of the bigger species.

Kath—catechu.

Kāṭhi—fuel: Syn. Sāhān.

Kaṭhor—obstinate; foolish.

Kaṭbuāo—to get confused; to be rigid with cold.

Kāṭi—a kind of outdoor game.

Kātik—the month of Kartik (October-November).

Kaṭikan—a small quantity; very little (Sant. Tun'; H. Tani; Beng. Ekṭukun).

Kaṭikan re—seldom; in a minute.

Kāṭkom / **Kāṛkom**—See Kāṛkom.

Kātlā—wooden bowl; to wear cloth over the breast.

Kāṭu—wooden shoe or slippers; the finger.

Kātu—knife (B. Chhuri).

Kāṭuā—the ends of a warp that has been cut off after weaving.

Kāu / **Kāuā**—crow (B. Kahu).

Kauṛi—a kind of game.

Ke—indeed; how wonderful?

Keād'—parrot; cry of parrots.

Kechā—to tear into small pieces; a piece; a fraction.

Kecho—burnt tiles.

Kedā—simple past tense suffix (transitive).

Ked-tāikenā—pluperfect tense suffix.

Kel—a village where there are a few houses: used as a name ending of villages, *e.g.*, Urikel, Simbukel, Ṭoṛangkel. The Hinduised and corrupt form of 'Kel' is 'Kelā' which is also used as a name ending of villages, *e.g.*, Dehkelā, Kisirkelā.

Ken—indefinite perfect participle suffix, *e.g.*, senken hoṛoko, the men who had gone.

Ken-tāikena—pluperfect tense suffix (intransitive).

Kenā—simple past tense suffix (intransitive).

Kendrā—a stringed instrument ; rudimentary violin.

Keṇted'—innumerable (B ; Very much ; difficulty ; impossibility).

Keo*n*ṭ—fisherman ; ferryman.

Keṛā—buffalo.

Keṛā—to call ; to invite.

Kerāyā—rent.

Kerkeṭā—a species of bird : a Munda sept.

Kero—a low-caste foreigner.

Kesed'—close ; tight ; to shut up ; to obstruct ; obstruction.

Keṭe—strength ; force ; hard ; blunt ; to strengthen.

Keti—to till, to cultivate (H. Kheti).

Khabar—news ; information.

Khabardār—to be on the alert.

Khachṛāhā—wicked.

Khādān—a quarry or mine.

Khājānā—treasury ; store room.

Khājānchi—treasurer.

Khālgi—a big leaf cup.

Khāli—empty.

Khamā—to forgive ; to remit.

Khānchā—a kind of big bamboo basket.

Khānchi—See Kanchi.

Khāṇḍā—sword ; to cut in two.

Khaṇḍi—a measure of grain : half a Kāṭ or 20 seers.

Khāṇḍit—a caste of Oriya Hindus.

Khāngār—Mundas of a lower status : also called Māhli, or Pātar.

Khāp—sheath of a sword.

Khāpāo—to fit up a covering or lid or cork.

Khāprā—tile : Syn Kecho.

Khārā—an instrument for levelling earth.

Kharchā—money for food (B.).

Khārdāni—See Kardhani.

Khāṛiā—an aboriginal tribe living in west Chotanagpur.

Khārij—to strike off.

Khaṭpat—inconvenience ; trouble.

Khāṭi—a kind of out-door game.

Khātir—to be patient ; consolation.

Khāwāsin—a concubine.

Khāwās—dealer in betel leaves.

Khechrā—anything badly done.

Khesāri—a kind of pulse (H., Beng.).

Khilāp—adverse ; against.

Khilā—a nail ; a pin to prevent anything from coming off.

Khipisi—reciprocal form of Khis.

Khiṛki—window.

Khirsi—soil mixed with sand and mud.

Khis—anger ; enmity : Syn. Kurkur (B. Kurkur ; H. Khis).

Khisāo—to be angry : Syn. Kisiāo.

Khis-tān-ko—enemies.

Khoā—condensed milk.

Khodā, **Kodā**—to tattoo.

Khogir—saddle.

Khongso, **Khonso**—hair-pin.

Khorām—to hammer.

Khub—very much.

Khuchrā—small coins.

Khunṭ—a social distinction among the Mundas originating in difference of duties in connection with village government. There are generally two

Khunṭs and sometimes three Khunṭs in a village—the Munḍā Khunṭ, the **Pāhān** Khunṭ, and the Māhto Khunṭ, and sometimes a Kuār Khunṭ. Khunṭs of a village are descendants of one and the same family.

Khunṭ kāṭṭidār—a descendant in the male line of any member of the family of the original Munda founders of a village, who reclaimed jungle lands, cut down forests and settled in the village.

Khurā }
Kurhā } —rinderpest.

Khusi—pleasure ; wish ; will.

Kiā—a small box for keeping vermillion.

Kichri—cloth ; B. ;

Kiki—to neigh (B. Hinha).

Kikir—a kind of bird.

Kilā—fort.

Kili—sept ; totemestic sept or clan among the Mundas.

Kili-hāgā—brethren of the same Kili or clan.

Kilimili—every sort ; various (B. Jāhān Kāhān).

Kimin—younger brother's wife ; son's wife.

Kin—sign of the dual number.

Kiriā—oath ; to swear.

Kiriā kānāe—to grow fat.

Kiriā jom—to swear.

Kiring—to buy (B., Sant., Sans., Beng. Kraya).

Kirsā toyā—milk of a recently calved cow.

Kisānṛ—cultivator ; master ; employer ; well-to-do ; honourable.

Kisiāu—to be angry with ; to chide.

Kisim—kind ; sort.

Kislā—adge : Syn. Bāsilā.

Kistā—instalment.

Kitā—date palm.

Kitā-rasi—palm juice ; toddy.

Kiuā—chin.

Ko—anterior future tense suffix to intransitive verbs.

Ko—plural suffix.

Koāsi—fog (Beng. Kuāśā).

Kobi—cauliflower ; cabbage.

Kochā—corner ; a compartment.

Kodā—to tattoo.

Kode—a kind of grain (H. Maṛua).

Kodom—a kind of tree. See Kadam.

Koilā, Kuilā—charcoal ; coal.

Kokā, Koki—deaf and dumb.

Ko-kombā, Ko-kombi—a funnel of leaves : Syn. Chongā.

Kokor—a kind of bird of the owl species : Syn. Dundu.

Kokrocho—the cry of a fowl.

Kol—a generic term applied to the Mundas and the allied tribes.

Kolom—threshing floor.

Kolom sim—the ceremony of fowl sacrifice on the threshing floor before paddy is threshed.

Kompāṭ, Konkpāṭ—Mundas of a high status.

Konā—corner : Syn. Kochā.

Konchā—a measure ; less than a pailā.

Konḍe—a small axe.

Ko*n*e—to beg ; to pray.

Konoe—petition ; prayer.

Kongso—hair-pin.

Kopā—to wipe off dust or impurities.

Koṛā—husband ; a male.

Koṛkār—reclaimed land; upland converted into low land by embankment or otherwise.

Koron-jo—a kind of fruit which is pressed for oil.

Kos—a measure of distance, equivalent to about 3 miles.

Kos-ko-so—silent owing to anger or peevishness.

Kosoṭ—pain.

Koṭā—to shake off dust from cloth.

Koṭāp-kārse—a kind of vulture.

Koṭāsi—a smaller hammer.

Koṭe—to hammer; to beat with hammer.

Koṭhā—ceiling of a room, where things are stored.

Koṭo—thin branches of a tree.

Koṭong—to intercept; to stop from proceeding.

Koṭwar—a chowkidar: Syn. Diguar, a 'Parha' official.

Kouā—crow: Syn. Kau.

Kouri innung—a kind of game.

Koyo—to peep.

Koyong—lap; to seat a child on the lap.

Kuā—a term used in the games of Chhur and Bhow*n*rā, denoting disqualification, corresponding to 'out' in cricket.

Kuār } —unmarried.
Ku*n*ār }

Kuār—the month of Āsin (September-October).

Kuchu—a bag.

Kuchlā—eel.

Kud—to hang a child on the back by wrapping it up with cloth.

Kudā—black berry.

Kuḍā—to roll up (B.).

Kudar don—best lowland.

Kudi } —broken grains of rice.
Khudi }

Kuhās }
Kuhāsi } —fog (B. Kuhuā).

Kui—a beef cup : Syn. Dulu.

Kuku—father's father's father ; also father's elder brother.

Kul—to send.

Kulā—tiger ; leopard (B.),

Kulāi—a hare.

Kulā uhur—Tiger skin ; a form of oath taken by the Mundas by touching the tiger-skin.

Kulhu—oil press : Syn. Gani.

Kuli—to ask ; to enquire ; enquiry.

Kuli uṛung—to enquire ; enquiry.

Kullām—a spade (Beng. Kodali).

Kum—leather oil bag ; a big earthen vessel.

Kumāng }
Kumāing } —mother's brother (B. Māmu).

Kumbā—a temporary straw hut created for the purpose of watching crops.

Kumhār—the potter caste.

Kumni—fishing net.

Kumṛu—to steal ; thief ; theft.

Kumṛu kumṛu—stealthily.

Kumṛu hār ipil—*lit.* bedstead thief star. The Ursa Major is so called.

Kumsing—a wooden fence ; a wooden barricade.

Kumu—to dream (B).

Kundām—back part of a house.

Kunḍṛi—a compartment.

Kunji—key.

Kunuli—question.

Kupul—guest ; visitor ; relation (B).

Kur—hoof.

Kuṛā—to roll up anything (Sant. Totro : H. Gutao).

Kurām—cheest (B. Kunduram).

Kuṛi—wife ; a female.

Kuṛid'—a species of hawk (Beng. Chill).

Kuṛi hon—girl.

Kuṛil' }
Kuṭil } —to jump ; extreme joy.

Kuṭukuṭu—uneven ; undulating.

Kurmi—a Hindu caste.

Kursi—a chair.

Kurtā—a kind of coat : Syn. Sono.

Kuru muṭu—in hot haste.

Kus—a kind of grass.

Kusal—welfare.

Kusti—to wrestle : Syn. Optā.

Kuṭām—hammer ; to grind (B).

Kuṭāo—to beat.

Kuṭāsi—hammer.

Kuṭhi—womb.

Kuṭi—a kind of tree.

Kuṭ-lā-hā }
Kuṭnā } —to go between ; an instigator.

Kuṭu—a miser.

Kuṭum—relation : Syn. Nata.

Kuṭung—to carry on the back : to hang on the back (B. Hochor).

Kutuṇṛi—pillow (B. Oṭhongā gāṇḍu).

Ku-u'—cough ; to cough.

L

Lā—past tense suffix signifying one past action over another (when the object is inanimate). It is really a contraction of the suffix ledā.

Lā—to dig with a spade superficially ; to slice off earth ; to cut grass with a hoe or spade (Sant. Lā—to dig deep). Mundari ur chālu—to dig deep.

Lāb—profit : Syn. Uḍungjāuā.

Lābānlubun—slowly (said of one walking) : Syn. Tāpā tupu.

Lābār hātnā—a species of forest tree (H. Arjun).

Lābdā, Lebdā—to throw ; to hurl : Syn. Hudumā.

Lābhāin, Lābhṛā—false ; to deceive : Syn. Hosoṛ (Sant Lābhṛā).

Lāblāb—quickly (said of one speaking).

Lāchār—helpless.

Lāchlāchā—shameless.

Lachmi—cattle.

Lācho—upper lip.

Lād—bread ; cakes of anything : to bake anything : Syn. Holong.

Lad, Lāi—belly.

Lādā—over and above : Syn. Lāgāe (H. Lābhsābh).

Lādi—to load (Sant., H. Lādnā).

Lādi poṭo—intestine (B., Poṭo).

Lādur ludur—slowly ; softly (as of one walking).

Lāḍu—a kind of ball-shaped sweetmeat (H. Lāḍḍu).

Lāphurā merom—a goat with long hanging ears.

Lāg—ill feeling ; disagreement.

Lāgātingā—*lit.* will have to ; will be required ; liability ; obligation : Syn. Hobāoā.

Lāgā—to become weak or tired or worn out on account of illness or any other cause ; to look tired.

Lāgāe—See Lādā.

Lāgāete, Lāgājānāete—having been tired out.

Lāgāo—to join ; to attach.

Lāgājānā—to become very weak on account of illness : Syn. Usujānā.

Lāgālāgi—adjoining ; close by : Syn. Ṅāñṛe ; Sāṭāoākān.

Lagantol—*lit.* to tie or fix the 'lagan' ; to fix a time for marriage.

Lāge } **Lāe** }—an exclamation, asking one to begin something.

Lāh—to peel off ; to cut off the surface : Syn. Lidu.

Lāhāk—to amuse : Syn. Rasikā.

Lāhāngā—a short loin cloth.

Lahasuā—a kind of song sung towards the end of the rainy season.

Lahrāo—to be inflamed.

Lāhṭi—armlet made of lac.

Lāi—belly ; stomach ; abdomen (Sant. Lāc').

Lāi-ā-kānāe—pregnant.

Lāihāsu—any bowel complaint.

Lāi sul—dysentery.

Lāj—shame ; modesty : Syn. Giu.

Lājāo—to be ashamed of.

Lājbhājāo—false : Syn. Hosoṛo.

Lakaṭ pakaṭ—mischief.

Lakhāo—to be visible ; to be known : Syn. Ṭhor.

Lākhṭā } **Lākṭhā** }—to quarrel falsely ; to entangle falsely ; to dispute falsely ; entanglement ; dispute.

Lākṛā—wolf (B. Rugṛa).

Lāl—a 'Pārhā' official ; a designation borrowed from the Hindus ; a younger scion of a royal family being called a Lāl.

Lālchā—greedy : Syn. Bukṛu.

Lālhār—fool ; rash.

Lālis—complaint.

Lālkāo—to amuse : Syn. Rasikā.

Lāloch—covetousness : Syn. Lob.

Lālsa lālsi—to accuse each other.

Lāmka—tell : Syn. Jiling.

Lāmpi—a hawk.

Lāndā—to laugh (Sant.).

Landar phandar—anything bad ; false ; got-up ; concocted ; mischief ; to create discord ; to ferment quarrel ; anything fraudulent. (Sant. Land-bhandao—to decay, to meet with adverse fortune : *cf.* Beng. Laṇḍa bhaṇḍa—disorder, ruin).

Lānḍi—buttock (B. Chutturā).

Lānḍiā—lazy (Sant. Landhia ; B. Koṛhi).

Lānḍiā tikin—10 A.M. (when people get tired in the field or when the lazy worker leaves the field : *lit.* lazy man's noon.

Lānḍhiā—lazy.

Lāndup—when the beams and rafters of a house have broken but have not fallen to the ground and the fall is broken by the walls, the house is said to be lāndup jānā.

Lāng-cheñṛe—a kind of bird with a long tail.

Langaṭ—naked ; penniless ; poor.

Lāng chāngiā—foppish ; dissolute.

Lāng lāng—a person whose cloth is so long that it trails over the ground.

Lāngṭā—Same as Langaṭ.

Lānkā—very far away ; distant ; any distant country, beyond the seas.

Lap—a handful (B.).

Lāpālis—complaint against each other.

Lāpārāi—reciprocal form of Larāi (B.).

Lāpāṭi—reciprocal form of Lāṭi.

Lāphāo—to stretch out the arm.

Lāphua—a species of bird that hops about.

Lāpkāo—to jump up to reach something.

Lāpos lopos- soft and over-ripe : Syn. Libur libur.

Lapṭāo—to get mixed up ; to roll up.

Lapṭā lapṭi—rolling or tumbling over each other : Syn. Lāṭilāpāti.

Lāpud—chicken-pox (B.).

Lār-bing—a poisonous serpent (*cf.* H. Lahar—burning sensation).

Lār—saliva ; a string of beads (Beng. Nal).

Lāṛāi—fight ; battle ; quarrel.

Laṛākā—prone to fighting.

Laṛ baṛāo—to stammer ; to get confused in speaking.

Laṛbaṛiā—a mischievous fellow.

Lārā cheñṛe—a lark.

Lāṛeā—crooked ; bent.

Larlarāo—loquacious and idle.

Lāṛu—tongue of a bell : Syn. Loṛho.

Lāṛum pāṛum—to masticate and move the food from one side of the mouth to another.

Lāsā—gum.

Lasgar—juicy ; good.

Laskar—a retinue ; a crowd.

Laslasā—sticky.

Lat—a creeper : Syn. Naṛi (Beng., Sans. Latā).

Lātā—a cave ; a hole or crevice (B. Lāt).

Lāṭāb—scissors (B.).

Lāṭāi—a thread winder.

Lātār—below ; down ; under (Sant., B.).

Lātār Guchā—beard.

Lāṭhā—bird lime.

Lāthiāu—to kick : Syn. Phādā.

Lāṭi—to turn down ; the ring on the upper part of the arm.

Lāṭi lāpāṭi—Same as Lapṭā-lapṭi.

Laṭkāo—to stick ; to hang.

Laṭlaṭ }
Laṭlaṭā } —sticky.

Laṭpaṭāo—rolled up and confused.

Lāṭum—mouthful (Sant. Lapeṭ).

Lāṭum—to fold.

Laukā—a boat.

Lauṛi—a small stick (Beng. Nori).

Lauṭāu—to return back : Syn. Ruāṛā.

Le }
Li } —future tense suffix (to transitive verbs) indicating priority of a future action, over another.

Le—abbreviated form of 'āle'.

Le—to melt ; to dissolve : fully saturated with water so as to feel soft to the touch.

Le-é—tongue : Syn. Ālāng.

Lebdā—to throw ; to hurl : Syn. Hudumā.

Lebe—soft (B., Sant. Lābit).

Lebed'—to press down ; to fill tightly.

Leber-Leber }
Libur-Libur } —very soft and over-ripe.

Leche-Leche—slowly.

Leche-peche—unsteady.

Lecher-pecher—muddy.

Lecho—to get blunted, as a weapon, by striking against some hard substance.

Led' }
Lid' } —excrement of animals.

Ledā—past tense suffix of transitive predicates, indicating one past action over another.

Lede lede—soft.

Leder beder—anything carelessly and badly done.

Leḍhā—crooked and bent.

Leḍhā kānā—to limp.

Ledrā lijā—tattered cloth sewn together (Sant. Kānthā).

Lege—expression used to direct any one to act quickly: Syn. Mār.

Legoe pegoe—very soft, so that one side yields to slight pressure while the other side bulges out.

Leje peje—soft and sticky.

Lejhrāhā } Lejhor }—immodest.

Lekā—about; like; similar: suffixed to other words to form adverbs.

Lekā—to count (Sant. Lekhā, *cf.* Beng. Lekhājokhā).

Lekā—like; such.

Lekā te—in this way.

Lel } Nel }—to see.

Lel āu } Lelāgu }—to visit; to look up.

Leledā—the bee-hive of the bee of the largest species.

Lele engā—a species of very large honey bee.

Lele rasi—honey of the Lele bee.

Lelo—to be visible; to appear.

Lel uṛum—to recognise.

Lembu—lemon.

Len'—to be pressed by a heavy substance, to bruise.

Lenā—Past tense suffix of intransitive verbs, indicating one past action another; also used as a simple past tense suffix in some cases.

Lenḍād'—leech; earth worm; intestinal worm.

Lenḍked'—one suffering from eye troubles; used as a term of abuse.

Lengā—left (Sant., H.).

Lenjer—weak.

Lenjhar—unfinished; residue.

Len len—to crawl on the belly (as earth worms) (Sant. Len).

Leong bing—a kind of non-poisonous snake (H. Harharia; Beng. Hele).

Leoṛā }
Lānṛ }—the male organ.

Leped—mouthful.

Lepen—to creep under the earth and hide as fishes and worms do.

Lepes—soft : Syn. Lebe.

Lere bere—insufficient.

Lergo—to eat (Sant.).

Ler leper—very soft and pliable like a creeper.

Lese pese—to laugh.

Lese lese—too wet ; muddy.

Leser—to speak quickly and sharply.

Leser ākān—sharp.

Leser—to sharpen (B.)

Leser diri—a hone.

Leser leser—very sharp.

Leṭe peṭe }
Lolo po to }—anything having no sufficient water in it (said of curry, field, etc.).
Leṭer peṭer }

Leṭhā—a false dispute.

Letho—slow ; lazy ; weak.

Lewā—sowing in mud : Syn. Āchāṛā.

Liblibia—soft.

Libir libir—same as Leber leber.

Lidi lidi—to spread out branches.

Lidu—to bend (inanimate).

Lidu—to peel off ; to cut off the surface.

Ligum—to chew the cud.

Lijā—cloth : Syn. Kichri.

Likā—a suffix used to indicate a future hour within the day, meaning 'after some minutes.'

Liki liki—to grow quickly.

Likir likir }
Lipir lipir } —to shake.

Liki piki—to be frightened (Sant.).

Lil—blue (H., Beng. Nil).

Lilā }
Nilā } —any show or tamasha (H.).

Lilāj—immodest ; shameless ; bad (H. Nilāj).

Lilām—auction ; to sell by auction (H. Nilām).

Limbud'—to throttle ; to press down (Sant. Limbot).

Lin'—to press ; to squeeze.

Lin-uṛung—to squeeze out.

Linḍā-hāi—a species of fish.

Lindar lāpār—trailing garment (either on account of being too long or on account of being torn).

Lingi—to flow ; to trickle ; to drop (Sant., B.).

Lipā—false.

Lipi—lark.

Kumbā lipi—bigger species.

Goeṭhā lipi—grey-coloured species.

Guia lipi }
Ṭāṭi lipi } —other species.

Lipin—reciprocal from of lin.

Lipir lipir—same as Likir likir.

Liṭi—to get bad (used with regard to food).

Lo—to burn ; to scald.

Lo—with ; along with (Sant. Salak).

Loā—fig.

Loād'—to moisten : Syn. Tupu.

Loā dāru—fig tree.

Loāri—morning meal.

Lob—temptation ; covetousness ; to covet.

Lobhāo—to tempt.

Lobhi—greedy.

Loboj—word.

Lochhon }
Lăchhan } —behaviour ; character.

Lochkor—lip.

Loch locho—to protrude the lower lip as a sign of disagreement.

Lodo—to look on wistfully while others are eating ; to look out for something hidden from view.

Lodo bhoso—stout and big-bellied (Sant. Lodgā).

Lodhor lodhor—very fat.

Loé—the male organ of generation.

Logo—to fascinate ; to cheat.

Logon—same as Lagan.

Logon tol—same as Lagan tol.

Lohā luti—iron implements and utensils : Syn. Meṛed′

Loh′me—a term of abuse, meaning ' die ' (Lo=burn).

Lokā—to catch in the hands (Sant., Beng. Loofā).

Lokā guṭi—a kind of game (Sant.).

Loko poko—large and fleshy.

Lolo—warm ; to warm oneself ; to heat.

Lolo dā—a kind of trial by ordeal by which the accused is made to dip his hand into boiling water and take out a coin thrown into it. Also used to mean semen.

Lolopoto—to pacify.

Lompoṭiā—licentious.

Lopo chopo—unreliable.

Lor—small streamlets.

Loṛo—to see, without being seen ; to lie in wait for ; to keep watch over one's coming.

Lorong phosong—faulty.

Losod′—earth ; mud.

Loṭ—currency note ; a handful.

Loṭā—a brass vessel for holding water (H.).

Loṭej′ }
Loṭoé } —to be sprained ; to sprain ; sprained.

Loyong—low land : Syn. Don.

Loyong bābā—paddy fit to be sown in low land; paddy ripening in November-December.

Lubhi—greedy : Syn. Bukṛu.

Lubui lubui—thin ; fine as grass.

Luchā—immoral ; licentious ; bad.

Ludām dāru—a kind of tree.

Lugā—cloth.

Lujhuk lujhuk—to walk with a load on both sides of the shoulder.

Lukhi }
Lokhi } —a brass cooking vessel.

Luku jono— a broom made of grass.

Lukundi—a young man who accompanies a bridegroom (Sant. Lumti), or a friend or companion of a betrothed girl.

Lulhua—back of the wrist.

Lum—to wet ; wet.

Lumāng—silk-worm ; cocoon ; silk.

Lumāng kārdhāni—a kardhani of silk thread.

Lunḍi—a wooden ladle.

Lunti—a kind of minute fly, said to cause ophthalmia : Syn. Putki (B. Terom).

Lunukuj'—wrist.

Lupu—husk of rice.

Lupu mui—a small stinking ant.

Lupu pusri—itches ; sores.

Lupung dāru—a kind of fruit-bearing tree (H., Beng. Baherā).

Lur—sense ; skill ; ability (Sant.).

Lur bing—a mythical serpent which is supposed to be poisonous and its breath is believed to produce the rainbow : Syn. Bānḍā lele or Bānḍāsiki (Sant. Athre bing.)

Luṭ—to rob : Syn. Re (H.).

Luṭā luṭi—struggling to grab ; to rob each other : Syn. Repe.

Luṭi—hank of thread.

Lutiā-luti—a very small insect which flies about in the daytime and is said to propagate ophthalmia: Syn. Putki (B. Ṭerom).

Luṭerā—robber.

Lukum—fat.

Luṭkum hāṛām } **Luṭkum buṛiā** }—The first human pair according to Munda cosmogony who survived the general rain of fire sent down on earth by the Sing Bongā to punish mankind for their sins.

Lutur—ear.

Lutur tukui—ear-boring ceremony.

M

Mā—a day (Sant. Māhā).

Mā ā'—to cut.

Mā'usar—to extend by reclamation.

Māchā—a raised platform (H.).

Māchi āndhā—nightfall, when it is not quite dark.

Māchi—border with a pattern.

Mād'—bamboo.

Madhe—middle ; from among ; between ; very seldom used (H.).

Mādkom—a kind of flower-bearing tree the flower of which is used for brewing liquor. *Bassia latifolia.* (H. Mohuā ; Sans. Madhukam).

Mād' sākam—a form of oath ; to swear by the bamboo leaf.

Mādoli
Mādli } —amulet ; charm.

Maeda—flour : Syn. Holong (H.).

Māe musi—mother's sister or mother-in-law's sister.

Māeṛa muhā
Māe ṛāhā } —one having little or no moustache.

Māg
Māgh
Māge } —The month of Māgh beginning with the new moon of the Hindi month of Pous when contracts for services are entered into for the new years.

Māgā—a kind of oil seed (H. Sargujā).

Māge porob—a festival celebrated on the full moon day in the Hindi month of Pous—when the spirits of dead ancestors are worshipped and the new year begins. It is the chief harvest festival of the Mundas.

Magrā
Mangrā } —ridge tiles of a roof.

Māgni—gratis (H.).

Māhā—last year.

Māhādeo—the Hindu deity.

Māhājan—a money-lender (H.).

Māhāk—smell ; odour (H.).

Mahal—a big house.

Mahalā—story of a house.

Mahārā—one who tends cattle ; the Ahirs are so called.

Māhāto—a village official of later origin.

Mahimāu—relations: Syn. Kupul, Peṛā.

Māhir—gentle ; quiet.

Māhit—neat ; handsome.

Mahjud'—ready (H.).

Māh kālom
Tor kālom
Sātom } —the year following next year ; two years hence.

Mahkup'—to abolish ; to postpone : Syn. Aosān, Hāpen (H.).

Māhli—Mundas of a lower status : Syn. Khāngār, Pātar.

Māhsul }
Māsul } —rent ; toll (H.).

Mahurā—poison : Syn. Bisi.

Māi—an expression used in addressing females.

Māil—an arrow without a head-cap.

Māj }
Mānjā } —centre wood (H. Mānji).

Māji—bug (Sant.).

Majuri—wages : Syn. Kamira gonong (H.).

Makāi—maize : Syn. Jonṛa.

Makdamā }
Makardama } —suit ; case (H.).

Mākhan—butter (H.).

Mākri—ear-ring : Syn. Phirki-lutur tukui.

Māl—rent ; goods (H.).

Mālā—necklace : Syn. Hisir (H.).

Malāo—to rub ; to massage.

Mālār—a Hindu caste ; those who make wooden pailās.

Māldar—wealthy ; owner : Syn. Mālik.

Mālguzāri—rent (H.).

Mālhān cheṇre—a kind of bird.

Māli—a gardener (H.).

Māli bāhā—a kind of flower.

Mālik—owner ; master ; wealthy (H.).

Malkāo—to amuse ; to make a show : Syn. Rāsikāo.

Māmā—mother's brother (maternal uncle) : Syn. Kumāing (H.).

Māmā bhāgnā—uncle and nephew (H.).

Māmi—maternal uncle's wife (H.).

Māmlā—a case or suit (H.).

Mān—honour ; respect (H.).

Man—a maund (H.).

Mānā—to forbid ; to remonstrate : to warn.

Mānārāng—(inspite of objections) resistance.

Mānāting—to obey ; obedient ; to heed ; to respect ; to propitiate ; to have faith in ; to desist from an act when forbidden.

Mānāting bongā—the household gods and the village gods who are worshipped periodically and on every auspicious occasion when their blessings are invoked.

Māndā—cold ; coryza.

Mānḍā—a foot-print ; a fair to set one's foot.

Mānḍā buru—a sacred hill ; a hill where fairs are held.

Mandan bher—a large trumpet.

Mānḍāo—to put on the ground ; to keep : Syn. Do.

Māndar—a drum : Syn. Dumang.

Māndariā—a drummer : Syn. Dumāng sāṛiko.

Mānḍi—boiled rice (Sant.).

Mā-ānḍi—to cook rice.

Mānḍi oṛā—kitchen ; cook-shed.

Mandil—a temple (H. Mandir).

Mānḍini—cook.

Mānḍowā—a temporary leaf pandal erected in the courtyard on the occasion of a marriage.

Mānḍowā baikoṛā—the young men who erect the Mandowa.

Mānḍowā dārom ṭākā }
Mānḍowā kesed' ṭākā } —The price, usually Rs. 1-4-0, paid by the bridegroom's party to the bride's party when a sham obstruction is placed on their way to the bride's Mānḍowa.

Mānḍowā-sim—fowl sacrificed on the occasion of the erection of a Mānḍowa.

Māne }
Māno } —meaning.

Māngal }
Kusal-Mangal } —welfare (H.).

Māngāo—to send for (H.).

Mangar—Tuesday (H.).

Māni—mustard.

Māniāḍār—a money order ; a corrupt form of the English word.

Māni-bā-bing—a python supposed to carry a jewel on its head.

Mānj }
Mānjā }—centre wood.

Mānjāo—to clean by rubbing.

Manjil—a day's journey.

Mājhi—a Sarawak caste of the Jaina community, speaking Bengali.

Mānjhi-hās—the landlord's priviliged land corresponding to 'khāmār' in Bengal.

Mānjhila—second.

Manjur—to agree ; to approve ; to accept.

Mānki—name of the ancient headman of a 'pāṛhā.'

Mānoā—a human being.

Mnasṛnā—a burial ground.

Mantar—incantation (H.).

Māp }
Māphi }—to forgive (H.).

Māp }
Nāp }—to measure ; measurement : Syn. Sonong.

Māprāng—very large ; great ; big.

Mār—quickly ; instantly : Syn. Lege.

Mār-he—all right, then ; come on, then.

Mārā—a peacock.

Mārāmat—to repair : Syn. Bābāi, Bāi-ruṛā.

Mārāng—large ; great ; big ; to become great ; head ; principal ; chief ; first-born.

Mārāng-buru—a big hill ; a fair or festival.

Mārāng ḍāḍo—thumb.

Māṛāo sunung—a medicinal oil.

Mārāng tiju—a kind of insect.
Mārāng ti kāṭu—thumb.
Mārā*n*ṛnā—a carrying pole (H. **Bāhingā**).
Marchā—fallow.
Marchi—pepper : chilly.
Mardāo—to rub the body.
Marde—an expression used in addressing colleagues.
Mār ge—now and quickly.
Mārghāṭi—a burial place or burning ground : Syn. Masnā
Mār-hege—emphatic 'yes.'
Māri—any deadly epidemic.
Māri—old ; aged.
Māri }
Māri guṭi }—small-pox.
Māri chāuli—old rice.
Māṛi māṛi—slowly.
Marjādi—to show respect ; respectable ; honourable.
Marji—will ; pleasure.
Markāo—to break (incompletely).
Mārkin—a kind of cotton cloth.
Mār mār—a species of centipede (H. Gojar ; Beng. Kennui).
Sengel mārmār—a kind of poisonous centipede.
Māṛom—a platform used to keep straw.
Mārsāl }
Māskāl }—light ; to light ; to emit light ; to shine.
Mārtul—hammer : Syn. Kutāsi.
Masālā—spices.
Māsgurā—gum ; boil.
Māsi—Moses.
Māskāl—see Mārsāl.
Maskāo—to subside.
Masmasāo—indisposed : Syn. Rasras.
Masnā }
Masa*n*ṛnā }—see Mārghaṭi.

Masrāo }
Pasrāo } —to spread ; to scatter.

Māsri—a kind of pulse.

Māster—school-master.

Mat—opinion.

Māt' }
Mād' } —bamboo (Sant.).

Mātā—mature, *e.g.*, fruit.

Matar—a kind of pulse : Syn. Batura.

Mātbar—old and respectable ; wealthy : Syn. Kisā*n*ṛ.

Māthāni—top or peak of a hill : Syn. Buru chuṭi.

Māthāsi—the upper portion (cover) of the pot for distilling liquor.

Mati—a witch-finder ; diviner ; one who finds out the causes of illness, etc., caused by spirits : Syn. Deo*n*ṛā ; So'khā.

Matlab—wish ; intention ; purpose (H., Beng.).

Maṭkāo—to be stuck.

Mat'kom }
Mad'kom } —a kind of tree the flowers of which are distilled for liquor (H. Mahua ; Sant., Sans. Madhukam) ; *Bassia latifolia.*

Mat'kam hāi—a kind of fish.

Mātwār—drunkard : Syn. Bul.

Maurasi—hereditary tenures.

Māyā—affection ; pity (H.).

Māyān muyun—to be alone ; solitary.

Māyāng—waist.

Māyi—expression used in addressing females younger in age than the person addressing.

Māyom—blood ; to bleed (Sant. Māyām).

Me—bleating of a goat.

Me—abbreviated form of 'am'—you—used as a suffix in the imperative mood, *e.g.*, Hiju me—(you) come !

Me āng—day after to-morrow (H., Beng. Parsu).

Mech—chair : Syn. Gāndu, Manchi.

Mecher mecher—to walk fast.

Mechkā mechki—to wink; to make signs with the eye (used always with respect to young lovers.)

Med'—eye (Sant. Met').

Med'dā—tears (Sant.).

Med'duku—disease of the eye; Ophthalmia.

Med'gāṛā—cavity of the eye (Sant.).

Med'ipil—pupil of the eye.

Med'kānḍom—eyebrow (Sant. Met'kuti).

Med'muāṅrā—the whole face ; countenance.

Med'pipni—eye-lashes (Sant.).

Med' rājā—the eye ball.

Mehāo—to fit ; to fix.

Mehnot—labour (H.).

Mehnotiā—industrious.

Mejāj—temperament (H.).

Mel—agreement ; harmony ; collusion (H.).

Melāo—to gain over.

Meme—a goat (in the language of the children).

Men—to tell ; to say.

Menā—to exist ; to be ; to be present ; as opposed to 'bānoā.'

Mendo—but ; on the other hand (Sant. Menkhan).

Menjādā—has said.

Mente—because ; on behalf of ; for the purpose of ; thinking it to be ; with a view to ; saying (this); to this effect ; used as an affix to form adverbs.

Mepen—reciprocal form of 'men'; to consult together, to speak to each other.

Merāl } **Merel** }—a kind of fruit-bearing tree : *Phylanthus emblica* (H. Aonrā ; Beng. Āmloki).

Meṛed'—iron (Sant. Merhet).

Meṛed soṭā—a stick bound with an iron band.

Mer gerāi—the joint procession of the bridegroom's party and the bride's party after their first meeting in the bride's village.

Merbāo—to twist; to wind.

Mer mer—exceedingly; very much: Syn. Kenṭed'.

Merom—goat.

Merom gupi dāṛi hon—*lit.* fit to tend goats; a boy aged ten.

Merom med'—a kind of plant (H. Gunj).

Merom oṛā—shed for goats.

Mesā—to mix; mixed (Sant. Mesal; Beng. Miśāna; Sans. Miśrita).

Mesed' mesed'—slowly: Syn. Māṛi māṛi.

Metā—to say; to call; to name.

Metāiā—said; will say; used both in the future and in the past tense.

Metād'koā—said to them.

Meṭāo—to wipe out.

Meṭ māṭ—to settle; to hush up (H.).

Meyād—term; period (H.).

Meyādi—terminable.

Miād', Mod', Moiād, Mid'—one; single: the difference being that 'Miād' applies to inanimate objects and 'Mid'' applies to animate objects (Sant. Mit).

Mid'ge—like one; equal; same (Sant. Mitge).

Mid' ghāṛi—a short while.

Mid'hisi—one score; twenty.

Mid' lāgāo—unceasingly; continuously.

Mid' lāi—uterine.

Mid' lekā—like one; similar.

Mid' mon te—with one mind.

Mid'sā—once; one side.

Mid' sāe—one hundred.

Mid' te—together; jointly: Syn. Mid're.

Mihin—fine.

Milān—to join.

Mil jul—agreement.

Mimid'—one by one ; singly ; one each.

Minḍi—sheep; one having shaggy hair ; Beng. Meṛā.

Minhā—to deduct.

Mirgi—epilepsy.

Miru—a parrot.

Misā—once ; a contracted form of 'Mid sa.'

Misā te—together; in company; at the same time.

Misā torsā—entirely ; completely ; suddenly ; without warning.

Misi—moustache: Syn. Guchu.

Misi—black tooth-paste.

Misi—sister (Sant. Miserā).

Misil—records of a suit (H.).

Misri—sugar candy.

Mistri—a mechanic or artisan (H.).

Miṭhā—sweet: Syn. Sibil (H.).

Miṭhāi—sweetmeat.

Mo }
Moā }—to swell; swollen (H.).

Mochā—mouth (Sans. Mukha ; Beng. Mukh.

Mochilkā—security bond (H.).

Mod'—same as Mid'.

Mode }
Monde }—to become mildewed ; mouldy.

Modet' }
Modod' }—to assist ; assistance : Syn. Dengā.

Moe—bud of a flower ; to bud (Sant. Mohe).

Mogoe—to smile.

Mogol—a Kabuli.

Moh'—pity; compassion (H.).

Moh'jud'—to collect ; ready (H.).
Mohni—to charm ; charm (H.).
Mohor—seal (H.)
Moi—to bud.
Moj rā—deduction (H.).
Mokāo—to become speechless.
Mokābilā—to confront (H.).
Mok moko—to be angry and silent with a puffed up mouth.
Mokodomā—a law-suit (H.).
Mokṛāri } —a perpetual lease (H.).
Mokṛorā }
Mol—price: Syn. Gonong (H.).
Molāim—smooth.
Molāo } —to polish ; to cleanse by rubbing.
Malāo }
Molāo—to repay in kind in satisfaction of a debt.
Molong—forehead.
Molong hāsu—headache.
Mon—mind; spirit (H.).
Mon—a maund (H.).
Mone—to wish ; to think ; to consider.
Mone ākādā—thought ; intended ; was about to.
Monṛeā—five.
Mon subā—wish ; real intention.
Mophsol—private (H.).
Morā—bundle of grain : Syn. Poṭom ; Tipsi.
Morābā—aloe.
Morjād—respect ; honour ; to respect (H.).
Morji—wish ; pleasure (H.).
Morlāhā—weak ; delicate ; incapable (used contemptuously).
Morso—to fade away.
Mosā—once.
Mosā mosā—sometimes ; now and then.

Mosā sirmā }—the year before year before last; two
Mosed' sirmā } years ago.

Tor mosed' sirmā—the year before 'Mosed' sirmā,' *i.e.*, three years ago.

Moskot'—to be spoilt by smoke.

Mosmoso—lazy.

Mosrāo—to eat like a glutton.

Moṭā }—fat; thick; coarse (H., Beng.).
Moṭo }

Moṭhāi }—by force; forcibly.
Moṭhe }

Moṭkuri—gravel: Syn. Rugud.

Mu—nose.

Muchi—a cobbler (H.).

Muchilkā—see Mochilkā.

Muchu—a kind of basket; a kind of fishing trap.

Muchur—crunching sound.

Mudai—complainant; plaintiff; enemy (H.).

Mudāle—accused; defendant (H.).

Mudām—finger ring.

Mugi dāl—a kind of pulse.

Muhā muhi—face to face.

Muhu—nose.

Muhni—a philtre.

Muhu unḍu—nostril.

Mui—ant.

Ṭonṭe mui }—Big-headed black ant.
Dāḍo mui }

Sunum mui—poisonous, biting ant.

Lupu mui—very small, stinking ant.

Hāo mui—large red ant.

Nidir mui—white ant.

Mujrā—to set off; to deduct (H.).

Mukā—to measure with the hand; a cubit, *i.e.*, the measure from the elbow to the tip of the middle finger.

Mukhiā—principal; chief (H.)

Mukunṛni—knee.

Mul—chief; principal.

Mulu—to reappear again (used with reference to the moon only; sometime jestingly applied to persons also).

Mulu chānḍu—new moon.

Munapha—profit (H.).

Mungā—pearl; red bead.

Mungā hisir—a necklace of red bead.

Mungā lumān—silk cocoons found on certain jungle trees.

Mungā—a necklace of red beads.

Mungāru—a wooden mallet.

Mungāru ipil—*lit.* hammer star. The Pleiades, so called from its shape like a cudgel or hammer.

Munḍ—head: Syn. Bo (H.).

Mundā—to close an opening: Syn. Teped' (H. Mudānā).

Munḍā—the Munda race; the headman of a Munda village.

Munḍāi—office of a headman.

Munḍāi pāwā }
Munḍāi don } —the land pertaining to the office of the Munda.

Munḍā munḍi—in equal portion.

Munḍi—end; meaning; truth; substance; to explain; to understand the sense of (*cf.* Beng. Muṅṛo.)

Mundhni }
Mundhnā } —the highest point of a roof.

Munḍlā—to crop the hair closely; a shaved head.

Munu—beginning (*i.e.*, of creation).

Muphut—gratis (H.).

Mur—principal (of a sum of money) (H.)

Murāi—radish.

Murchhāo—to cut off evenly and roundly.

Murdār—a corpse; often used contemptuously, meaning a coward.

Murdān—untouched food.

Murkh—peevish; ignorant and obstinate.

Muṛli—a bamboo flute.

Murud'—a kind of lac-bearing tree (H. Parās; Beng. Palās), *Butea frondosa.*

Murum—a kind of deer.

Musing—one day.

Musing bārsing—one or two days; a day or two; a short time; a few days.

Musing musing—occasionally; sometimes.

Muskil—difficulty (H.).

Musṛā—a club used in beating down flat the bundles of paddy when being tied up.

Musri—a kind of pulse.

Muṭh—the measure of the distance from the elbow-joint up to the palm closed up (Sant. Mudrā).

Muṭhi—handle; a handful.

Muṭhiāo—to grasp tightly.

Muṭkā—to strike with clenched fist.

Mutul—ridge pole of a roof.

Mutukul—first-born; first sent; primary.

N

N—in poetical languages "N" is placed before a word beginning with a vowel, *e.g.*, Nāchur for āchur, in Ipil nāchur jānā—the stars have risen.

Nā—expression used in addressing very near relations, *e.g.*, daughter and mother.

Nā—now; this time (Sant. Nahak).

Nājā'nā—any.

Nā-ā-do—now ; however.

Nā-āh'—just now ; this time.

Nā-āe—this man.

Nā-āte—from this time.

Nā-e-ke—sometime after (within the course of the day).

Nā-hābe—till now.

Nā-jaked—hitherto.

Nā-sān-te—as yet.

Nabāb—rich and haughty (H.).

Nābālok—minor ; minority (H.).

Nāchā—false hair used as a hair tape.

Nāchāo—to cause to dance (H.).

Nāchār }
Lāchār } —helpless (H.).

Nāchni—a dancing girl of low caste (H.).

Nāchu—a small bamboo basket.

Nāchur—poetical form of āchur, to rise ; *e.g.*, Ipil nāchur jānā.

Nāḍā—lower portion of the stem of the paddy plant, which is left uncut (Beng.).

Nāḍi—a creeper.

Nāg—a species of snake ; a sept of the Mundas.

Nagad—cash (H., Beng., Sant. Nogod).

Nagar—city ; town.

Nāg-hing—same as Nāg ; a species of snake.

Nāg-nāgin—male and female Nāg spirit (evil).

Nāge ārej ghāo—white leprosy ; supposed to be due to water having been sprinkled on the body of the diseased person by the Nāge-bongā.

Nāge bongā—Nāge spirit.

Nāge dā—reddish coloured stagnant water, supposed to be due to the Nāge erā residing there.

Nāge erā—the spirit presiding over marshes.

Nāgen
Nāgente } —for ; with a view to (Sant. Lagit ; Beng. Lagi).
Nātin

Nāgeṛā—a large drum ; to announce by beat of drum.

Nāgor—mew of a cat.

Nāgrāhā—one who lives in towns.

Nāgṛāhā—sticky mud soil.

Nāel—the wooden frame of the plough into which the 'Pāl' or iron ploughshare is inserted.

Nāelgāḍā—furrow.

Nā-enāng—by this time ; up to this time.

Nāhāk—fruitless ; useless (H.).

Nāhān—bathing ceremony connected with birth, marriage and death.

Nahsr—water channel.

Nāi—a big river.

Naihar—parent's house (H.).

Najar—to see ; sight ; view (H., Beng., Sant. Najor).

Najarbund—to confine.

Nājom—witch (Sant. Nāujom).

Nājom duku—a wasting disease said to be caused by witchcraft.

Nā-kabul—to deny (H.).

Nakal—copy ; to copy ; to sham (H., Beng.).

Nākāṭiā—snub-nosed ; one whose nose has been cut or destroyed in any way.

Nāki—comb ; to comb.

Nāklāhā
Naklāhi } —pretender.

Nākṛā hāsā
Nāṛkā hāsā } —a kind of earth used as soap, to wash the hair.

Nāksā—map ; picture.

Nākṭā—snub-nosed.

Nāl—horseshoe ; bullock shoe ; tube ; pipe (H.).

Nālā—rivulet ; stream ; wages of a labourer.

Nālis—complaint ; to complain (H.).

Nām—to get ; to obtain ; to seek ; to find ; to search also added as a suffix to other verbs.

Nām āu—to search out and bring.

Nām bāṛā—to search about here and there.

Nām uṛung—to search and find out.

Nām jādi—famous ; notorious (H. Nāmjādā).

Nāmni—one who searches.

Namunā—pattern ; sample (H.).

Nām ruṛā, **Nām ruāṛ**—to get back ; to recover.

Nān—thin ; fine (Sant. Nanhā).

Nānā—elder sister ; mother's father.

Nānā honjār—grand father-in-law.

Nānām ni—one who finds or gets.

Nānāporkār—various ways ; various kinds (H.).

Nān bir—a thin jungle.

Nānā rakam—various kinds (H.).

Nāndān—poor ; weak ; powerless ; to slight.

Nāṅḍe—close by ; near.

Nā*n*ḍe hā*n*ḍe—hither and thither.

Nā*n*ḍi—creeper (Sant. Naṛi).

Nāgos—to hate.

Nānhe—slender ; thin (H. Nan).

Nāng—a remote period.

Nāng ko pariā—ancient times.

Nāngāli—the string used in a plough.

Nā*n*ṛe—close by ; near.

Nāni—grand mother : Syn. Aji, Jiāng.

Nāo—boat (Beng.).

Nāoki—a she-buffalo which has not yet calved.

Nāp—survey ; to measure : Syn. Song.

Nāpāe—vigorous ; healthy ; absence of discord.

Nāpām—reciprocal form of Nām ; to meet together.

Nāphā—profit (H.).

Nāpaṛh—illiterate : Syn. Ḍonḍo.

Nārā-durā—weak ; convalescent.

Nārāj—to displease; to be displeased (H.).

Narak—hell ; dirty.

Naram, **Narmā**—soft : Syn. Lebed'.

Nārāng-nurung—to grumble ; to be dissatisfied ; to beg importunately.

Nārāngi—orange.

Nāṛi—a creeper ; a plant.

Nāṛ joṛ, **Nāt got**—relationship by marriage.

Nar singā—a brass or copper trumpet of long size.

Nās—to waste ; to destroy ; to ruin (H.).

Nasdāni—a small box for powdered tobacco ; snuff-box.

Nasib—fate (H.).

Nasṭ—to destroy.

Nātā—relationship.

Hāturā nātā—village relationship, irrespective of caste, assumed for the purpose of addressing each other.

Nāti—grand child.

Nāṭā—dwarf.

Nātiā—relationship between wives of brothers (Beng. Jā.).

Nath, **Nathni**—nose ring (H.).

Naṭ khaṭiā—naughty ; rogue (H.).

Nauā—a barber (H.).

Nau*n*ṛā—mongoose.

Nawā—new ; fresh (H.).

Nāwāi—to offer the first fruits to the Sing Bongā.

Nāwā-khāni—festival in connection with the eating of the first crop : Syn. Jom-nāwā.

Ne—take this (vocative).

Ne—this.

Neā—this thing.

Neā—this one (inanimate).

Ni—this one (animate).

Neā-ge—this very.

Ne ākin—these two (inanimate).

Nikin—these two (animate).

Ne āko—these (more than two) (inanimate).

Niko }
Niku } —these (more than two) (animate).

Ne-ā-te—by this ; with this ; by means of this.

Ne-betar }
Ne-s-kān } —this time ; this occasion.

Nekā—in this way ; in this wise ; in this manner.

Nekān—such.

Ne-kālom—this year.

Ne-lekā }
Nekā }
Ne-lekā-te } —in this way ; thus ; this wise ; like this.

Ne-re }
Newre } —here ; in this ; inside this ; in this place.

Ne-re-ā—the one of this place (inanimate).

Ne re ko }
Ne renko } —those of this place (animate).

Ne re ni—the one of this place (animate).

Nesā—this side ; this direction.

Ne s kān—this time (Beng. Ekhan).

Ne tāiom te—after this ; hereafter.

Netāre }
Ne te re } —on this side.

Neāe—to judge rightly (H.).

Neār—ceremony of purification ; to purify oneself by ceremonies (Beng., Sans. Prāyaśchitta).

Neār—to fast and purify oneself on the day previous to the day of worship (Beng., Sans. Saṁyama).

Neār en—to purify oneself.

Neār-i—to purify another.

Ned'—to dye ; to colour.

Neḍā } —to fix a time ; a fixed time ; due time ; due season.
Nenḍā }

Neech—low ; mean (H.).

Neg'—ceremony ; rule ; ordinance.

Nehāl—to fail to do ; unable ; unsuccessful.

Nehāit—very ; a mean-minded person.

Nehoor—to bend down and entreat.

Nel } —to see ; to look ; to consider ; (Sans., Beng., Nīrikṣaṇa).
Lel }

Nel-ād'—to fail to recognise ; to lose sight.

Nel āgui me—go and see and come back.

Nel āsrā—to expect anything (H. Umed).

Nel āu—to come along seeing.

Nel choṭe—to have a glance.

Nel dārom—to welcome.

Nel-ḍhilāu—to neglect to see ; to neglect.

Nel-eṭā—to mistake one for another.

Nel-god'—to see one depart ; to see for a moment ; to catch a glimpse.

Nel-goe'—to see one die.

Nel hārā—to see one grow up.

Nel horā—to expect one coming.

Nel-idi—to go along seeing ; to go and see back.

Nel jom—to see one eating ; to enjoy a sight.

Nel-kedā—saw.

Nel lā—had seen.

Nel nām—to see and find out.

Nel nel—to see, for the purpose of seeing.

Nel okā—let it be seen.

Nel umbul—mirror ; a looking glass.

Nel uṛung—to recognise ; to see and choose.

Ne-mān—near about the place ; hereabout ; in this place.

Nemar—meek ; gentle ; good-natured (Beng., Sans. Namra).

Nem-dharam—chastity.

Nenel—reduplication of Nel ; to look repeatedly; sight for the purpose of seeing.

Ne-nel-ko—seers ; prophets.

Neo—foundation.

Neo-chhar—to sanctify ; to purify.

Neotā—invitation.

Ne parom— on this side.

Nepel—reciprocal form of Nel ; to see each other ; an acquaintance.

Nepel re—in view of ; within sight of each other ; within visible distance.

Nepel umbul—mirror.

Nepel upṛung—an acquaintance.

Nepeotā—reciprocal form of Neotā ; mutual invitation.

Nerā—see Neḍā.

Netā ete—from this place.

Netāra—(those) of this place (inanimate).

Netāre—here ; in this place.

Netā ren—(those) of this place (animate).

Net dharam—way of living ; conduct.

Nete—on this side ; hither.

Ni—a suffix used to form nouns.

Ni—this one (animate).

Ni-āte—with this ; by means of this.

Nibar—weak.

Nibhāo—to spend time (H.).

Nibrāo—to complete ; to finish (H. Nimrāo).

Nichuṛā—to squeeze.

Nichit
Nichint } —free from care or anxiety ; careless (H.).
Nichut'—noiseless.
Nichut'-te—noiselessly.
Nidā—night ; last night.
Nidāmed'—night-blind.
Nidānubā—dark night.
Nidāo—to become night.
Nidariā—fearless.
Nidir—white ant (Sant. Nindir).
Nidrā
Nidrālu } —sleepy.
Ni-ēte—from him.
Nihāi—anvil (H. Nehāi).
Nihāit—mean ; low ; to hate ; to despise.
Nihāit—absolutely mean ; low ; to hate ; to despise.
Nij'—to open.
Nij—one's own.
Nijāt—without any caste ; outcast.
Nijgut—exactly ; certainly.
Nijhar—pure ; clear : *cf.* Sans. Nirjhara.
Nijuān—adolescence.
Nikās—outlet.
Ni-ke—him (pointing to the man).
Niki-badi
Neki-badi } —good and bad.
Niking—these two (animate).
Niko
Niku } —these (more than two) (animate).
Nilājiā—shameless.
Nilām—to sell by auction ; auction sale (H.).
Nijhāo—to extinguish (H.).
Nijhar dā—pure water.
Nim—a kind of tree, *Azadirachta Indica*.

Nimān—pure; limpid (Sans. Nirmala).

Nimak hārām—ungrateful; disloyal (H.).

Nimin (ne-imin)—this much; this number (animate).

Nimināng—just this much (inanimate): Syn. Nāmināng.

Nimin huṛing—so small.

Nimin jāked'—up till now.

Nimin mārāng—so big (pointing to something).

Nimin sānte—up till now.

Nimpiṛāng—this little; this trifling amount.

Nimṭāng (Ne-imtang) (Na-imtang)—this very time; presently; now.

Ninās—breath (H., Sant. Nisas; Beng., Sans. Niśvāsa).

Nindā—to blame.

Nindir—white ant.

Ninghā, Nigha—axle (Sant.).

Nipaṭ—near.

Niphor, Niphuṭ—not separated; joint.

Nipṭāo—to complete; to settle (Sant.).

Nipun—skilled; expert (Beng., H., Sans.).

Nir—to run; to run away; to flee.

Nirāl—beautiful (Sant. Niral—pure).

Nirās—to be disappointed (H., Beng.).

Nir-bāgi—to run away leaving something behind; to desert.

Nir-bāk, Nirbachan—speechless (Sant., Sans., Beng., H.).

Nirbas—untractable.

Nirbans—childless.

Nirbisrā—the period just before the rainy season (from Mṛgaśirā, a constellation in Hindu astronomy, in which the sun enters in June. It is believed that the season is so hot and dry that even the snakes lose their poison during this period and deer shed their horns).

Nirbolo—to run and enter; to run into.

Nirbodh / **Nirbudhi** }—foolish (Sant., Sans., Beng. Nirbodh).

Nirbuj—slow to understand.

Nirdae—pitiless (Sant., Sans., Beng., H.).

Nirdand—free from care.

Nirdhan—poor (Sans. Nirdhana).

Nirdok / **Nirdos** }—innocent; faultless (Sant. Nirdos; Sans., Beng. Nirdoṣī).

Nirghin—one who is hated; hateful; dirty.

Nire-hujul—to run slowly and trotting.

Nirjān-chānḍu—the moon which has disappeared, *i.e.*, last month.

Nirmuchiā—a person who has no moustache.

Niroḍong—to run out.

Nir-susun—a kind of running dance, in vogue during the Sarhul festival: Syn. Senojān chānḍu.

Nisā—any intoxicating substance.

Nisān—sign; mark (H.).

Nisā-te—on this side.

Niskapaṭ—sincere (Sant., Beng. Akapaṭ).

Nispiṭar—Inspector.

Nisṭā—exactly; truly.

Nisun—void; soundless (Sant., Sans. Śūnya).

Niulā—this day; this time.

Nit—every day (Sant., Sans. Beng., H. Nitya).

Niti / **Net** }—conduct; dealings.

Niyār—see Neār.

Niyat—settled; fixed (Sant. Nit; Sans. Niyata).

Nohor-nohor / **Nogor-nogor** }—to grumble; growling of a dog.

Nokoe—poetical form of 'okoe.'

Nokar }
Chākar }—servant (H., Beng. Chākar).

Noksān—damage ; loss ; to damage (H., Beng. Loksān).

Nolād'—lampblack ; soot.

Noth—nose ring.

Nu—to drink.

Nubā—dark (Sant. Nut).

Āyub-nubā—dark night.

Nudum—twilight (Sant. Nuhun).

Nuidā—drinking water.

Nui-lekā-lolo—sufficiently hot for a drink.

Nukui—poetical form of 'ukui.'

Num }
Nutum }—name ; to name ; to call by name (Beng., H., Sans. Nām).

Nunu—breast.

Nunuā—to suckle.

Nunu-bāle }
Nunutān-hon }—an unweaned child.

Nuputum—reciprocal form of Nutum.

Nur—to flow out (said of non-liquid substances such as sand or any grain as opposed to 'lingi' applied to liquids).

Nurā—to cleanse cloths ; *lit.* to strike against a hard substance.

Nurung-nurung—delicate ; feeble ; growl of a dog.

Nutum—name ; to name.

Nutum-do neg'—name-giving ceremony.

Nutum-kāhāni—a riddle.

Nutum-marang-o—to exalt ; to praise.

Nutum-sāki—to name a child after its grand-father or maternal uncle.

Nutum-te—in the name of.

O

O—suffixed to a word to mean 'too,' 'also,' 'even,' 'in addition to.'

O—exclamation of anger, regret, despair, or distress.

Oā—house (in the language of children).

Oār—to skim out by the hand.

Oāri—verandah (H.).

Oāris
Oārisdār }—heir (H.).

Obor—to lie down on the belly; to fall flat on the belly; to couch on the belly (as a leopard); to screen oneself from view.

Obrā-ubri—having the belly of one person, touching the belly of another.

Ochā
Ocho }—to stand apart; to detach; to move away; to remove.

Od'—to cut off by one stroke.

Odā
Odā-modā }—damp; moist; wet (H. Oda).

Odāsi—whey; churned curd.

Oḍo
Hāḍo }—and; more; moreover; in addition to.

Oḍong—to bring out; to extract; to find out (from a place out of the view); to come out.

Oed'—to contract the stomach (Sant. Orsech').

Ogrā—watchman.

Ohāe—cry of an infant.

Ohdār—diku headman of a village.

Oho
Oh're }—an exclamation of sudden surprise.

Ohrāo—to subside; to decrease.

Oiji—in place of; substitute.

Oiyār—to swim ; swimming.

Oiyārinung—a kind of game.

Ojhā—witch-finder ; a magician : Syn. Māṭi (H., Beng.).

Ok'—to vomit ; to throw up : Syn. Ulā-uṛung.

Oko—which ; what.

Okoā }
Okon } —which one (inanimate) ; some thing.

Okoākin—which two (inanimate).

Okoā-re—in which thing.

Okoā-reā—in which thing is that (inanimate).

Okoā-re-koā—where are those things.

Okoe—who (singular) from Oko-ae—who ; he (animate).

Okoe-ā'—whose (singular, animate).

Okoe-okoe }
Okoeteko } —which one among you ; the person who.

Okoe-o—even one.

Okoe-tā-king—which two persons ?

Okoe-tāko—who (plural).

Okoe-tākoā—whose (plural).

Oko-hulāng }
Chi-hulāng }
Chi-ulā } —what day ; when.

Oko-king—which two (animate : except in the case of man) ; some two.

Oko-ko—which ones (animate : except in the case of man) some ones.

Oko-lekā }
Chi-lekā }
Chilkā } —what like ; how.

Oko-neā—which one (inanimate).

Okoni—which one (animate) ; some one.

Okoniking—which two ?

Okoniku—which ones ?

Oko-re—in what ; in what place ; where ; (re-in, on).

Okore-okore—wherever.

Okoreā—of what place (inanimate) ; where is that (inanimate).

Oko ri ā—of what place (animate) ; where is that one (animate).

Okoreko—where (are) they (animate).

Oko sā
Oko sāe } —which side ; which direction.

Oko tā—what place.

Oko tāre—in what place ; where.

Oko tā jāked'—up to what place.

Oko ṭāid
Okoṭhāoṅ } —what place ; which place.

Oko te
Ok te } —to which side.

Ol'—to write ; to draw ; to make a drawing or pattern.

Ol'—to get cracked.

Ol—a kind of edible root.

Olādiṇāe—he wrote to me.

Oltā diṇāe—he wrote for me, or on my behalf.

Ola kādā—has been written.

Olākād' tāikenā—was written.

Olā kānā—is written.

Olā kān—cracked.

Ol jānā—has been written.

Ol kedā
Ol-lā } —wrote.

Ol-ked'ni—the man who has written.

Ol-ledā
Ol-lenā } —had written.

Olni—writer.

Ol tānā—writes.

Om
Em } —to give ; to pay.

Omāini—the person who is given.

Ombā—the cry of calves.

Om e āh—gift.

Omni—the giver.

Omo'—generous.

Omon—to germinate (Sant.).

Om rikā }
Om-tukā } —to make to pay; to make to give.

Om-tukā—see Om-rikā.

Oñḍkā—one who kills human beings (as a sacrifice) by cutting the throat (Sant. Oñḍga).

Onḍor—to kindle fire.

Onoḍong—outlet; place of egress.

Ong'—to breathe into; to blow with the mouth.

Onol—writing.

Onol }
Bāni } —stripped; coloured.

Oñṛñā—to get sour and stale and unfit for consumption.

O-od'—to rub the body with water, by the hand.

Opād—a sapling (Sant. Opat').

Opoḍo—to add more eatables on each other's dish.

Opor—reciprocal form of Or; to drag each other.

Optā—reciprocal form of **Ota**; wrestling; pressing down each other.

Opun }
Upun } —four (Sant. Pon: *cf*. Beng. Pan $=4 \times 20$).

Opun-mā—four days.

Opupuniā—four each.

Or—to pull; to draw; to drag.

Oṛo—and; again; etc.

Oṛā }
Oḍā } —to lie down in mud.

Oṛā—a house; to build a house.

Oṛā-bongā—spirit of the house.

Oṛā dur—house and hearth.

Oṛā gomke—master or mistress of the house ; wife.

Oṛā hoṛo—wife (Beng. Gṛhiṇī ; H. Gharni : Syn. Oṛā gomke).

Oṛā-renko—members of the house.

Oṛa-kundam—back of a house.

Bangla oṛā—a bungalow.

Chatom oṛā—house.

Girjā oṛā—church.

Giti oṛā—the sleeping house.

Gonṛā oṛā—the cow shed.

Iṭā oṛā—brick-built house.

Kaed oṛā—jail.

Koṭhā oṛā—a two-storied house.

Kuṛiā oṛā—dormitory.

Khaprā oṛā—house with tiled roof.

Losod' oṛā—a mud-walled house.

Māndi oṛā—kitchen.

Merom oṛā—shed for goats.

Rānu oṛā—hospital.

Sāuṛi oṛā—a thatched house.

Thānā oṛā—police station.

Uri oṛā—cattle shed.

Oran'—to drag.

Oṛe—bird.

Oṛeā—a bamboo basket-maker.

Oṛej'—to crack; to tear ; to rend ; to split into pieces ; first ploughing (H. Chirnā).

Oṛiāo—to arrange ; to set in order.

Or jālom—a drag net.

Oṛo—still ; once more ; and ; again : see Oḍo.

Orong—to blow ; to play a flute (Sant. Oron).

Osār—broad ; wide (Beng.) ; to widen ; to stretch.

Osar—a heifer.

Otā—to squeeze; to press down; to pounce upon, in the manner of a beast of prey (*cf.* Beng. Ot—to lie in wait).

Oṭā—to uncover; to open, *e.g.*, a book (Sant. Oṭak; H. Uṭka).

Oṭāngo—to be carried away by wind.

Ote—ground; field; land; world; earth; soil; floor of a house.

Ote bir }
Ote sān }—holding (H. Tagah jamin).

Bugin ote—fertile soil.

Buru ote—hill soil.

Diri ote—stony soil.

Gitil ote—sandy soil.

Gurguḍi ote—gravelly soil.

Lobo ote—muddy fertile soil.

Sārā kān ote—manured soil.

Usar ote—barren soil.

Ote disum—earth.

Oṭej'—to spring up (as when paddy grains are fried).

Oṭo—knot (*e.g.* of a bamboo or reed.).

Otong—to follow.

Oṭongā—same as Ondkā.

Oṭhngāo—to prop up; to lean upon.

Otong tāni—one who follows; a follower.

Otong topol—to follow one after another.

Oṭom ṭorom—miscellaneous articles.

P

P—inserted in verbs to indicate the reciprocal form, *e.g.*, Om-opom, to give to each other; Nel-nepel, to see each other; etc.

Pā-ā' }
Bā-ā }—flesh or meat, in the language of children.

Pabitā—the papaya fruit.

Pabitar dā—holy water.

Pāchak—digestive.

Pāchan—a particular manner of weaving cloth.

Pachāo—to digest; to consume; to appropriate.

Pāchar—to tighten by inserting a piece of wood (*e.g.*, in the hole of a handle).

Pāch-gāndu—to sit cross-legged (Sant. Paṭgando).

Pāchim }
Pāchhim } —west: Syn. Singi-ayub-sā.

Pāchlā }
Pāchhlā } —hinder part of any thing.

Pāchli }
Pāchhli } —to move backwards.

Pachmāhā—western.

Pāchri }
Bhit } —a mud wall.

Pādā-pādā—movements of the legs of a baby

Pādā }
Phādā } —to kick; to kick in the air.

Pādna M. }
Pādni F. } —one who passes winds.

Pādṛi-gomke—the priest.

Pāe—blemish; deformity; ill-omen.

Pāe-hā }
Pāe-ākān } —sickly; ill-omened (said of animals).

Paedā—produce; to give birth to.

Paesā—pice; money.

Pagār—an elevated ridge with a drain on one of its sides.

Pāhāl }
Pā-āl } —iron ploughshare.

Pāhāñṛ—the village priest or sacrificer in a Munda village.

Pāhi }
Peṛā }
Kupul } —a guest.

Pahichān—to recognise.

Paham—to remember; to think; to consider.

Pāhrā—a guard; to watch: Syn. Horo.

Pāikāṛ—a retail dealer.

Pāikhā—a kind of dance; one who dances the 'Pāikhā' dance.

Pāilū—a piece of cloth used to cover the breast.

Pailā—a measure of grain; a wooden vessel for measuring grains.

Paiñchā-āu—to borrow.

Paiñchā-em—to lend.

Pājhrā—a spring of water: Syn. Seteng, Ḍaṛi.

Pāji—mean; despicable.

Pākā }
Pākāpāki } —final; definite.

Pākhā—a niche used in a wall as a shelf.

Pākṛe—one having a deformed leg.

Pal }
Palak } —twinkling of an eye; a moment: Syn. Rāpid' (H.).

Pālak-āṛā—a kind of spinach.

Pālki—a palanquin.

Pālhāo—sprouting of new leaves after the branch of a tree has been cut.

Palṭan—an army (H.).

Pālwā—dried tamarind leaves powdered and used as a condiment.

Pān—betel-leaves.

Pānā—molasses dissolved in water.

Pānā-dā—sweetened water.

Pānbharā—the assistant of a Pahan, whose duty is to carry water for the Pahan on ceremonial occasions; the land held for the above service to the village community.

Panch
Panchāit } a body of arbitrators for decision of social disputes.

Pāṇḍā—a vaccinator.

Pāṇḍe—a writer ; an adviser.

Paṇḍit—a learned man ; a guru (Sans. Paṇḍita).

Pāṇḍil
Phāṇḍil } —to rebound.

Panḍṛā—a buffalo (of greyish colour).

Pāṇḍu—grey-haired.

Pāṇḍubing—the cobra.

Pānich'—a bow-string of bamboo.

Pāñk-hāsā—sticky mud, free from sand.

Pān-khokhā—armpit.

Pāñk-loyong—good muddy soil.

Pān-khāwās—one who distributes lime and tobacco at a pāṛhā feast.

Pāntā—a line ; a row.

Pāntā-pānti
Pānti-pānti } —in a line ; in rows.

Pāñṛki
Putām
Dudmul } —a dove ; a pigeon.

Pāntinir—a kind of game.

Pāp—sin (Sans. Pāpa).

Pāpi—sinful.

Pāpṛādāru—a kind of fruit tree.

Pāṛ—coloured border of a cloth (H.).

Parab
Porob } —a festival (H.).

Paramesor—God (H.).

Pāṛāpāṛite
Pāṛipāṛite } —by turns.

Parchā—a preliminary record of rights ; loosely used for the finally published record of rights.

Parchār—a catechist; to preach (H.) (Sans. Pracāra).

Parchi } —clean; clear; to purify; purification.
Pharchi }

Pardesi—a foreigner: Syn. Diku.

Pardhān—a chief.

Parganā—division of a country (H.).

Pāṛhā—a unit consisting of a number of villages exercising social authority over its members.

Paṛhāo—to read; study (Beng. Paḍā; Sans. Pāṭha).

Pāṛhā panch—a fixed body of arbitrators in a Munda pāṛhā which decides social disputes.

Pāṛhā pāhān—the religious head at a 'pāṛhā' feast.

Pāṛhā-pānḍe—the convener of a 'pāṛhā panch.'

-Pāṛhā-rājā—president of a 'pāṛhā' panch in the Bhuinhāri-area.

Parhar } —clean; clear.
Pharhar }

Pariā—time; period (Sans. Paryāya).

Paṛia—a long piece of cloth worn by Munda females.

Pāriāo } —to settle; to decide; to make clear.
Phariāo }

Parjā—a raiyat; a tenant.

Parjātiā—of other castes.

Pārkār—kind; variety (H.).

Pārkom—stringed bedstead.

Pārkom-ipil—*lit.* bedstead star; the Great Bear is so called.

Pārom—across; beyond; on the other side; to go across.

Paṛosi—a neighbour (H.).

Parpan—clean (H.).

Parsād—to engage in friendship; friend (H.).

Partāp—power; courage; influence.

Pās—side.

Paṛti—fallow; uncultivated.

Parwān —a notice (H.).

Pasar
Pasri } —to graze cattle in the morning.

Pāse—to entrap; to catch in the net.

Paseri—a five-seer weight (H.).

Pāsi—a low-caste Hindu.

Pasind—to approve; to prefer; to like; choice (H.).

Pāsir—to be scattered, as by falling on a hard substance.

Pāskā
Pāsur } —to throw up earth by kicking (as by an animal).

Paskāo
Gaskāo
Phuchkāo } —to slip away; to escape.

Pās*ng*ā—to equalize the balance by putting some weight on the scale.

Pasrā—a smithy; to work in the smithy.

Pāsrāo—to spread; to extend.

Pasri—see Pasar.

Pasri—to work as ploughman in return for loan of plough cattle.

Pasridār—one who ploughs in Pasri. The custom is that the Pasridār ploughs his own field one day and in the alternate days he has to plough the field of the owner of the bullocks.

Pasu—animal.

Pāsur-pusur—to whisper.

Pāt—a wedge driven into anything to tighten it.

Pāṭā—a deed; a document.

Paṭāo—to irrigate (H.).

Pāṭmuṇḍā—the president of a 'Pāṛhā panch' in the Khunṭkaṭṭi area.

Paṭed'—inverted club-foot.

Pāthrā—a stone cup.

Pāṭhrā-poṭhrā—hustling or grappling each other.

Pāṭi—leaf mat.

Patias—to believe; to listen; to obey (Sans. Pratīti).

Pātiā-merom—a she-goat.

Pāṭiā-sukuri—a she-hog.

Pāṭidiri—a broad flat stone.

Paṭkā-paṭki—to throw each other on the ground (H.).

Pātrā—a jungle.

Pātrā
Pātri —leaf plate.

Paṭṭi—the name given to a 'Pāṛhā' unit by the Chota-nagpur state.

Pāṭub'—to throw (Sant. Pāṭup).

Pātwāsi—ornament for the head.

Pāwā—a measure; legs of a bedstead or chair.

Peādā—a peon.

Peāju—onion.

Pear—to love: Syn. Dulāṛ.

Pech—screw; a difficult situation (H.).

Pechā—owl: Syn. Ḍundu, Kokor (H.) (Beng. Peṅchā, Sans. Pecaka.).

Pechāng—to overflow.

Pechhouri—a single wrapper.

Pechkas—a screw-driver (H.).

Peko-poko—swollen cheek.

Pel-pel—very thin.

Pendā
Pindri
Pendari
Piṛingi —bottom; the base of anything.

Penhāo—to induce a cow to let down the milk.

Peṅṛāi—a semi-aboriginal weaver caste.

Penṭor—to twist; to twist and break.

Peṛā—a relation or kinsman; to receive and show hospitality to a kinsman.

Nepel-upṛum-peṛā—an acquaintance.

Nāñṛe-ren-peṛā—a near relation.

Sāngin-peṛā—a distant relation.

Nij-peṛā—a blood relation.

Gotiā-perā—a kinsman of the same caste.

Jom-mu-perā—a kinsman with whom partaking of food is permissible.

Peṛe—strength; might; ability; to be able.

Pereṛeñd—a long trumpet: Syn. Narsingā.

Pes—to present a petition.

Pesen-pesen—to ooze out in small quantities.

Peskār—a court official whose duty it is to present petition to the judge.

Peṭposā—selfish and greedy.

Peṭe—to twist and break.

Peṭej′—chaff.

Peṭi—a bamboo basket with a lid.

Peṭo—green; unripe; egg.

Peṭu—greedy (H.).

Phāchāk-phuchuk—to go about here and there.

Phāda } —to kick.
Pādā }

Phādil—a large level area.

Phāedā—benefit; profit; advantage.

Phāel—broad; wide

Phaelāo—to widen: to extend.

Phāgu—a festival celebrated on the full-moon day of Phāgun, borrowed from the Holi festival of the Hindus to signify the approach of the Vernal Equinox.

Phāgu-Chānḍu—the month of Phāgun (March-April).

Phāgu-parab—same as Phāgu.

Phajet—to trouble; to rebuke; to prosecute; worry.

Phalkāo—to break up the earth by ploughing.

Phalnā—a certain one; so and so.

Phāltu—extra; surplus.

Phāndā—a noose or trap; to ensnare.

Phāndāo—to bind together; to join together.

Phāṇḍil—to spurt out; to fly off, *e.g.*, a piece of wood, when being cut, or a piece of metal when being hammered.

Phāñk—open; open space.

Phāñsi—a noose; to kill by hanging.

Phārā—a piece; to cut up into pieces.

Pharchā, **Pharchi**—pure; clear; distinct; to clean; to clear up.

Phareb—false; to deceive.

Pharhar—clean; clear.

Phariāo—to settle; to decide.

Phārkā—to separate; separate; different; to remove; to get away.

Phārkān—at a distance; off; away.

Phārkāo—to separate; to take away.

Pharmāo—to give an order.

Phaṛ phaṛāo—to talk glibly; to chatter.

Phaṛ phaṛiā—a glib talker.

Phāsād—difficulty; trouble.

Phāsāo—to entrap; to entangle in trouble; to be in illicit love.

Phāsur phusur—to whisper.

Phāṭak—gate.

Phaud—a large assembly; an army.

Phaudāri—criminal; relating to crime.

Phechkā—a syringe.

Pheder-pheder—confused; jumbled together.

Phenṭor, **Penṭor**—to writhe and twist; to twist and break.

Pheṭāo—to mix up; to beat and mix.

Phikir—endeavour; solicitude.

Phiri—a shield.

Phitā—a tape.

Phiṭkiri—alum.

Phodā—the game of hockey.

Phodi—a kind of outdoor game.

Phodlo—worm-eaten wood.

Phohm, **Pohm**—to recognise; to remember.

Phokā—blister (Beng. Phoskā).

Phoki—(*lit.* empty) lac from which lac insect has escaped; unfit for use as seed lac.

Phokto, **Pokto**—good; strong.

Phokṭiā, **Pokṭiā**—humourous; also used in a bad sense, meaning vulgar, light-hearted.

Pholok—soft.

Phong—to be washed away by rush of water; to have an opening or oultet.

Phophuḍā, **Phuphunḍā**—rotten; mildewed; mouldy.

Phoṭāo—to hit a ball (*e. g.*, in hockey).

Phuphā—father's sister's husband.

Phuphu, **Hātom**—father's sister.

Phuchiā—a small earthen pot, used as a measure for liquid substances.

Phuchkāo—to slip away; to escape.

Phudnā, **Phudinā**—an ornamental cotton band worn round the waist or arm, with a portion hanging down as a pendant.

Phukār—to call; a call, referring especially to the calling up of cases in court.

Phuknari—a bamboo blow-pipe.

Phukur-phukur—to breathe heavily.

Phul—a ceremony by which two persons of the same sex engage themselves to friendship, by oath.

Phuphunḍā—see Phophuḍā.

Phur—to throw out of the mouth.

Phurti—quickly (H.).

Phursat—leisure (H.).

Phuslāo—to entice; to flatter; to coax; to lead astray (H.).

Phuski—to whisper.

Phusur-phusur—whisperingly.

Phuṭ—to break; to separate; to be divorced.

Phuṭāo—to break; to burst.

Phuṭā-phuṭi—separate; separately.

Phuṭia—small coins; copper pieces.

Piakaṛ
Piankaṛ } —a drunkard (H.).

Pichhā—to follow up; to search.

Pichki—a species of Colocasia.

Pichhouri-lijā—a wrapper-cloth, consisting of two pieces sewn up in the middle.

Piḍil-piḍil
Phiḍil-phiḍil } —to move the legs and hands briskly (*e.g.*, by a baby).

Piḍga-Piḍgi—to frisk about.

Pilhi—spleen.

Pilni—a kind of fishing net.

Pilsin
Pinsin
Pinsil } —a corrupt form of the English words pension or pencil; pension; pencil.

Pinḍā—altar.

Pindā
Piḍingi } —veranda of a house.

Pio-chenṛe—a kind of singing bird.

Pipā—a barrel.

Pipni }—eye-lashes.
Med'-pipni

Piṛhi }—a generation.
Piṛi

Piṛi—upland ; Syn. Ṭañṛ.

Pirit—love.

Piṛit'-piṛit'—dazzling ; shining.

Pirthi—the world : Syn. Ote-disum (Sans. Pṛthivī).

Pit—the gall ; bile : bilious.

Pitar }—bell metal.
Pital

Piṭhāo—to beat ; to hammer.

Pi-ṭ' }
Piṭh }—bazar ; market.
Piṭhiā }

Piṭi }—a bamboo basket with lid.
Peṭi

Piṭu—a glutton : Syn. Bukṛu (H., Beng. Peṭuk).

Piṭid'—to card cotton ; carded cotton.

Piuṛi—rolls of cotton to be spun into thread.

Poā—to break into small pieces.

Poe }—any malignant disease.
Pāe

Poetā—sacred thread (now used by some Hinduised Mundas).

Pokhrā—a tank : Syn. Bāndā.

Pokos }—soft : Syn. Lebe.
Pokso

Pokot }
Pokto }—good ; strong.
Poktā }

Pok-poko—swelled ; puffy.

Polā—toe ring.

Ponḍe—rotten ; dirty.

Poṇḍe-dā—uncleaned water.

Pongoe—to fly off with a sound (*e.g.*, an arrow).

Porob / Parab—a festival; a festive occasion.

Porbosti / Parbasti—to bring up; to nourish: Syn. Asul.

Porchā / Parchā—a record of rights.

Porchār / Parchār—to preach; a preacher; a catechist.

Poṛho—a species of fig, of the smaller kind.

Pormesar—God.

Poṛoe-poṛoe—thin; fine.

Pos—to nourish; to cherish; to bring up: Syn. Asul.

Porsād / Parsad / Parsādi—food that has been offered to the deities.

Posāo—to grow; to yield a return; to increase (*e.g.*, in the case of money lent on interest).

Posrā—to hate; to look down upon.

Posu / Pasu—an animal or beast.

Poṭā—to flay; to be bruised; intestines.

Poṭhā hāi / Chirpi hāi—a kind of small fish (Beng. Pūṭhi).

Poṭom—bundle; package; to make a bundle; to wrap up in a bundle.

Poṭpoṭo—a disordered or flatulent stomach.

Poṭrāo—to grasp round with both arms: Syn. Hāmbud'.

Powā—one-fourth seer.

Prachār—to preach; a preacher.

Prachārak—a preacher; a catechist.

Projā / Parja—a rāiyat; a tenant (Sans. Prajā).

Prati }
Mi-mid } —each.

Prerit—(*lit.* one sent) an apostle : Syn. Kulbeni.

Prithvi—the world (Sans. Pṛthivī).

Puchār }
Puchhār } —to ask ; asking ; seeking ; to enquire.
Khoj-puchār }

Puḍu—fried paddy grain.

Pudinā—a kind of plant leaf used as a condiment.

Pui }
Puhi } —peacock's feather or quill used as a float for fishing.

Puḍui-puḍui-dā—drizzling rain.

Pugṛi—private gain.

Pujā—to offer sacrifice ; to worship.

Pukār—see Phukar.

Pul—a bridge.

Pun—virtue ; merit.

Punḍi—white.

Punḍi-sud'—white leprosy, believed to be caused by the Nage-era Spirit.

Punḍit—a teacher ; a learned man.

Puni—infantile wasting disease.

Punji—capital ; savings.

Purā—entire ; full ; very many ; great ; the whole.

Purab—east.

Purānā—old ; ancient (H.).

Purānti—to complete a demand ; the balance required to make a payment in full satisfaction.

Purāni—a daily or periodical supplier.

Purāo—to complete ; to fulfil ; to pay in full.

Purbiā—easterly.

Purchāo—to say distinctly.

Puṛid'—to boil ; to boil and foam.

Purkhā—an elder ; ancestors ; a generation.

Purnā—old.

Purohit—a priest (H.).

Puṛu—a leaf-cup of small size.

Puṛu-puṛu—ebullition.

Purus—husband : Syn. Koṛā.

Pursā—a measure equal to the height of a man with upraised hands.

Pus—the ninth Hindu solar month.

Pusi—an eruption of the skin which is ripe for bursting ; to cause to burst.

Pusi—a cat.

Pusiko—a smaller species of crane.

Pust—a generation.

Pusri—itches ; pimples.

Pusur-pusur—to whisper.

Putām—a pigeon ; a dove.

Puthi—a book.

Puṭi—to flow out of a spring.

Puṭi dā—a spring.

Puṭ kui—fungus ; mushroom (round ball-sized) : Syn. Ud′-utu.

Puṭli—an image.

Putri—a kind of tree.

Putrid′—to get foamy ; froth (Sant. Pher).

Puyu-puyu—here and there.

R

Rā—possessive suffix (inanimate).

Rā′—to call ; to cry lowly ; call ; cry of any beast or bird. Sant. Rak′. *Cf.* Prov. Beng. Rā—call ; reply. Sans. Rava—cry.

Rā′-nā—weeping.

R-ā'-āu—to call and bring ; to call hither : Syn. Keṛā-an.

Rā'-hunḍi—to call together.

Rā-ruṛā—to call back. The second visit of the bridal pair to the house of the bride's father after the marriage.

Rābāi-rubui—to walk slowly.

Rābāl—light weight; as opposed to Hambal—heavy; easy.

Rābāng—cold ; to feel cold ; cool (Sant. Raban) ; to be light; to deliver ; to give birth to.

Rābāng sā—the cold season ; winter.

Rabāṛ—corrupt form of the English word 'rubber.'

Rabi—winter crop.

Rābrābā—of a coarse and thickly quality (said of salt or sugar).

Rāch—the comb of a loom through which the threads of a warp are passed through.

Rāchā—court-yard in front of a house.

Rāchā-ā—to clutch ; to pull ; to draw (*e.g.*, water).

Rāchā-āu—to drag and bring.

Rāchāre—outside.

Rāch-rāchā—tight and tense.

Rāḍ }
Rāḍahā } —scoundrel ; wicked ; greedy.

Radbadāo—a rustling sound.

Raddi—useless ; bad ; waste.

Rāe—opinion ; advice ; decision.

Rāg—musical note ; tune ; air.

Rāgāe-rāgāe—rough ; uneven.

Ragbāgāo—to move ; movement.

Ragad }
Ragdāo } —to rub.

Ragdā-ragdi—to rub.

Ragṛāo—to threaten ; to chide. (H.)

Rāh'—ordering some one to stop ; stop ! (H.)

Rāhāṛi
Rā-āṛi } —a kind of pulse (H. Rahaṛ) ; *Cajanus sativa.*
Rāheṛ

Rāi—mustard : Syn. Māṇi.

Rāilāgidi—a kind of vulture.

Rāj—kingdom ; ownership (of a moderately big area of land) ; to reign.

Rājā—a king ; a landlord.
Medrā-rājā—pupil of the eye.

Rājāi—to reign.

Rājāmāṇṛ—a Rajput.

Rāji—to agree ; to be satisfied ; to be pleased : Syn. Suku ; to settle a dispute.

Rājināmā—compromise ; agreement.

Rājon bājon—pomp and music.

Rākāb'—to rise ; to ascend ; to appear ; to lift up ; to hold up ; to offer up, as a sacrifice.

Rākāṛ rokoṛ—to make a rattling sound.

Rākas—a giant ; a demon.

Rākhā
Rākhāt } —reserved ; preserved.

Rākhijāgāo
Jāgāo } —to save ; to lay by.

Rākhwār—guard : Syn. Ogrā.

Rakṭāo—to be mad with rage.

Rālā rālā—very much.

Rāmā—nail ; claw.

Rāmāl bābā—a kind of lowland paddy which ripens early.

Rāmbṛā
Rāmbāṛā } —a kind of pulse : *Phaseolus Roxburghii* (H. Uṛid).

Rām singā—a long horn or pipe giving a monotonous sound.

Rānākāb'—rising ; ascent ; appearance ; a rising ground.

Rāndā—to plane ; a plane.

Rāndi }
Rāṅṛi } —a widow (H.).

Rang—colour ; to dye.

  Arā-rang—red colour.

  Hende-rang—black colour.

  Lil-rang—blue colour.

  Pundi-rang—white colour.

  Sasang-rang—yellow colour.

Rāngā—coloured ; earring.

Rāngāo—to colour.

Rāni—a queen.

Rāṅṛi—widow.

Rānu—medicine.

  Ili rānu—a kind of preparation used to ferment rice-beer.

Rānuni—a medicine-man ; a doctor.

Rāpā—to roast on fire.

Rāp rāpā—bristling hair.

Rāpid'—twinkling of an eye.

Rāpud'—to break : Syn. Foā (Sant. Raput'—to cut and make a breach).

Rāṛā—to loose ; to unbind ; to let down ; to open.

Rāṛān—act of setting free.

Rāṛe—to be cold : Syn Reāṛ.

Ras—sap ; juice ; soup.

Rasāo—to tinker ; to solder.

Ras baste—carefully ; willingly (Sant. Rache bache te).

Rase rase—slowly ; lẹisurely (*cf.* Beng. Roye-soye).

Rasi—rope ; soup ; juice.

Hurum suku rasi—honey.

Rasid }
Rasdi } —a receipt.

Rasikā }
Raskā } —to amuse ; to be happy ; to be pleased , mirth ; gay ; joyful ; to rejoice ; to be glad.

Ras-ras
Rasāo } —to be indisposed; to be ill on account of over-eating.
Ras-rasi

Rāstā—road; path: Syn Horā.

Rasuni—garlic.

Ratam dāru—a kind of tree.

Ratang—dew; mist; hoarfrost.

Rāṭā pāṭā—to lie in confusion.

Raṭ-raṭ—to make a creaking sound.

Re'—to rob; to snatch away; to take by force.

Re—in; on; upon; after: if; used as a conditional clause suffix; used as a locative suffix.

Reā—of; about; concerning; regarding; possessive suffix (inanimate).

Re-o—in that also; even these.

Reāṛ—to bathe; bath: Syn Reāṛen.

Rebed'—to insert; to thrust; to stick into.

Red'—slender root of a plant; root; to take root.

Redo—but; on the other hand; if it be so; if it so happens; used as a conditional clause suffix, *e.g.*, Ka redo—or else (Sant. Remā).

Reghā reghā—staircase.

Rejisṭāry
Rojosṭāry } —to register; registered.

Regṛāsākom—a kind of bracelet.

Rejki—small coins (H.).

Rel—rail.

Remet'
Rembed' } —a part of the intestines; to squeeze; to press.

Ren—possessive suffix (to common or proper nouns): used as in suffix to cardinal numerals, *e.g.*, Irāliā-ren hoṛo—the eighth men (animate).

Rended'—to get jammed; to crush (Sant. Riḍet).

Renge—hungry ; poor ; to be hungry ; to be poor ; hunger ; famine.

Ren-i—of (he) ; *i.e.*, he belongs to ; the wife of (when suffixed to the name of another person) : suffixed to cardinal numerals converting them to nouns, *e.g.*, āpiā reni—the third (one).

Renjed′—closely situated.

Ren-kin—of (two), *i.e.*, they (two) belong to.

Renko—of (more than two), *i.e.*, they (more than two) belong to ; the family of.

Re-o—even if.

Repe—reciprocal form of 're' ; to loot each other ; to struggle with each other for looting.

Repeko—robbers.

Repenjed′—close to each other ; crowded.

Reṛā, Reṛān—to bathe : Syn. Um′.

Rere-in—thief.

Resed—narrow ; narrowness ; distress.

Ret, Reti—a file.

Reṭhā-kāṛkom—a small crab.

Rewāj—custom ; usage (H.).

Ribi ribi—slowly ; by measured steps.

Richāp′, Ruchāp′—to pull off.

Richi—a hawk ; the hill near the Ranchi lake is called Richi buru ; many hawks are to be found there : hence the name Ranchi. The hamlet near the hill is the original Ranchi village. It is still called the Purānā Ranchi.

Rid′—to grind ; to crush ; to gin cotton.

Rij, Rijh—desire ; choice ; pleasure ; satisfaction.

Rijhāo—to satisfy.

Rijhuā—merry ; light-hearted.

Rikā—to cause to do ; to seek to do ; to arrange ; to force to do : used as a causative suffix.

Rim—to raise up ; to lift

Rimil }
Rimbil } —cloud ; to be cloudy.

Ringi-chingi—multi-coloured ; fine (*cf.*, H. Rangchangiā).

Riṛni—debt ; loan ; to borrow.

Ripi ripi—to wink.

Ripid'—to wink both eyes.

Riṛin }
Riṛing } —to be lost ; to forget.

Risā }
Risā-risā } —curled (*e.g.*, hair).

Risā-sim—a fowl having curly feathers.

Ris risi—ruffled.

Riṭhā—a kind of tree, the fruit of which is used as a substitute for soap for cleansing cloths.

Ro—to singe ; to burn the hairs of an animal preparatory to chopping it up for boiling.

Roā—soul ; spirit.

Roā—to transplant (Beng., Sans. Ropaṇam).

Roā kān—transplanted.

Rochod'—to break ; to crush any dry substance by pressing or trampling.

Roch-rocho—very thin.

Rod }
Rad } —to cancel.

Rod'—to tie up the hair and insert one end, so as to bulge out on one side (applied to males) ; in the case of females the word 'Supid' is used, which means, to tie up the hair with a pin or band ; to arrange and bring together what is scattered ; to make a covenant.

Rod'-pāṇḍu—grey haired ; very old.

Rog—disease ; illness ; epidemic : Syn. Duku.

Rohni—Aldebaran ; the constellation of Rohini of the Hindu astronomy in the sign of Taurus. The sun enters Rohini in the month of June, hence Rohini signifies the season for dry sowing.

Rohṛ—to dry ; to become emaciated.

Ṛohṛnājom—emaciation or illness supposed to be due to the effect of witchcraft.

Rohṛ kāṭā—the space between the ankle and the knee joint.

Rohṛ ti—the lower arm (from the wrist to the elbow joint).

Roj—daily (H.).

Rojgār—to earn ; earning (H.).

Rojgāriā—one who earns.

Rok—to prevent.

Rokā—ready ; sudden.

Rokāge—sudden ; instantly.

Rokāo—to prevent ; to obstruct ; to stop ; to interrupt ; to detain.

Roko—a fly (Sant. Ro).

Rokom—manner.

Rokot—blood : Syn. Māyom.

Rokṭok—obstruction ; impediment.

Rol—rent.

Rolā dāru—myrabolan tree.

Rolājo—myrabolan fruit.

Rom chom
Rombā chombā } —many-branched.

Rombod'—to seize with the palm and press on the ground.

Rond khond—topsy-turvy.

Rongo—to be burnt (said of anything sticking to the pot while being cooked).

Ropā }—to transplant : see Roā.
Roā }

Ropok—reciprocal form of 'Rok.'

Roṛ—see Rohr.

Roṛā—gravel : Syn. Rugud'.

Roṛ ces—corrupt form of the English word road-cess.

Roṛsud'—a kind of leprosy believed to be caused by the Nāge-erā.

Roṭe—frog (middle-sized).

Bārundā roṭe—a toad.

Sasang bārundā roṭe—a yellow toad.

Tuturiā roṭe—a small frog.

Roṭod'—pigtail knot.

Ru'—to beat : Syn. Dāl ; to beat a drum.

Ruā—fever ; to be ill of fever.

Pāre ruā—tertiary fever.

Ruāṛ—to return ; to cause to return ; back again ; ploughing of a land for the second time ; used as a suffix, *e.g.*, Kāji-ruāṛ—to reply ; Om-ruāṛ—to give back ; Bāi-ruāṛ—to repair.

Āu-ruāṛ—to bring back : to get back.

Hiju-ruāṛ—to come back.

Idi-ruāṛ—to take back.

Kāji-ruāṛ—to reply.

Jiu-ruāṛ—to come back to life.

Om-ruāṛ—to give back.

Rā-ruāṛ—to call back.

Sen-ruāṛ—to go back.

Rub'—to fall off, *e.g.*, hair, teeth, etc.

Rubā—to pick up with the hand.

Rud rudu—erect rough hair.

Ruji—the female organ of generation.

Rugṛi—a fungus.

Rugud'—gravel.

Rui-rui—rapidly.
Rukhaṛ—dry boiled rice (*i.e.* without gruel).
Ruknā—chisel.
Ruku—to shake.
Rul-uṛung—to bring out of the fire.
Rum′—to swing the head violently under obsession.
Ruṇḍā—a wild cat.
Rupa-ḍiḍi—the legendary silvery vulture.
Ruṛāng—to pierce.
Ruṛu—to leave in peace.
Ruṛun—to be fatigued ; to be tired ; to rest after fatigue.
Ruṛung—to husk rice in a dhenki ; to pound in a mortar.
Rusā rusi—to be sullen towards each other.
Rus rusu—to have a shivering sensation.
Rutā dāru—a kind of timber tree : *Polyalthia cerasoides*, Benth (H. Panjan).
Ruṭu—bamboo flute.

S

Sā—side ; edge ; times ; season ; towards.
 Gāḍā sā—riverside ; towards the stream.
 Hānsā—that side.
 Jeṭe sā—hot season ; summer.
 Mid′ sā—once.
 Ne sā—this side ; this time.
 Rābāng sā—cold season, winter.
Sā-re—with ; towards.
Sā-te—with ; towards ; to.
Sā-ān } **Sāhān** }—fuel ; fire-wood.
Sā-ār } **Chiāri** }—arrow (Sans. Sharam ; Beng. Shara).
Sāb′—to catch hold of ; to seize ; capture (Sant. Sāp).

Sāb′-idi—to seize and carry off.

Sāb′-ruṛā—to catch and bring again.

Sābā—dregs ; remains of anything after being strained or boiled ; insipid ; tasteless ; unleavened.

Sābāb—reason ; cause.

Sabad—voice ; sound : Syn. Sāri.

Sabhā—council ; assembly, meeting : Syn. Dunub′.

Sābit }
Sābut } —proof ; to prove.

Sābṛo—crow-bar.

Sābut—see Sābit.

Sabur—patience, to wait.

Sāchā—a mould.

Sadāe—always ; continuously.

Sadāgar—a trader, especially a cloth merchant.

Sādān horo }
Sādān } —a non-Muṇḍā ; a foreigner.

Sādāo—to press ; to give trouble to. See also Sātāo.

Sādhāran—common.

Sādhu—a mendicant ; a religious man.

Sāḍhu }
Sāṛhu } —relationship between the husbands of sisters.

Sādom—a horse.

Bāndhuā-sādom—a big horse that is kept in a stable.

Engā-sādom—a mare.

Ṭāṭu-sādom—a horse of short height.

Sādom-mui—a large red ant.

Sādom oṛā—a stable.

Sāe }
Sāo } —a hundred.

Sāe-jāng—the bones of the rib ; ribs.

Sāe-sāe—to look askance.

Sāe-sui }
Sān-sun } —lonely ; silent ; soundless.

Sāetān—Satan (H.).

Sāgā—prickly ends of certain grasses (H. Chorant).

Sāgā-ore—a kind of small bird living in bushes.

Sāgā-runḍā—a species of wild cat.

Sāgā-bāgā—closely packed.

Sāgāe sāgāe—rough and prickly.

Sāgāi—a form of marriage of widows.

Sāgāl sāgāl—numerous ; many.

Sagaṛ, **Sagṛi**—a cart with solid wooden wheels.

Sagaṛiā—driver of a sagar.

Sāgen, **Sāngen**—to bud ; to sprout.

Sāgu dānā—sago.

Sāgui-bagui, **Sāgur bagur**—disorderly ; in confusion.

Sāgum sugum—noiselessly ; stealthily.

Sāgun—omen, usually good.

Sahāe—to help ; to aid : Syn. **Dengā.**

Sāhāitā—help ; assistance.

Sahaj—easy : Syn. **Rābāl.**

Sahan, **Sa-an**—fire-wood ; fuel.

Sahao, **Sah-ting**—to bear ; to endure ; to suffer with patience.

Sahar—town (H.).

Saheb—a European (H.).

Sahi—signature to sight (H.).

Sahiā—a sworn friend (H.).

Sahiari—friendship (H.).

Sahil, **Saili**—a wild buffalo.

Sahrāo—to praise ; to thank.

Saiad—to breathe hard, as in fear ; to pant ; to sigh ; breath

Saidba—a kind of flower.

Sāikā—a fixed rent in kind.

Sāili—see Sāhil.

Sājāi—to punish ; punishment.

Sājhā—together ; in common ; in partnership (applied to leases of lands settled on half produce).

Sāji-hāsā—fuller's earth : used as a substitute for soap.

Sākā }
Bālā sākā } —the relations of the bride, or the bride-groom so called by the other party.

Sākam—leaf (of a tree or of a book).

Sakam he—to pluck leaves.

Sakarkāndā—sweet potato.

Sakat—hard ; strong.

Sāke—a thin jungle, but consisting of big trees.

Sākhā—conch-shell bangle.

Sākam-chhāri—the ceremony of divorce.

Sākhi—witness ; namesake ; the ceremony of naming a child after one of its ancestors.

Sākhi }
Sāking } —to make friends between persons of the same name ; a friend ; a companion.

Sakhṛi—dirty bits of food, grains of rice, etc.

Sākid'—to condense ; to evaporate ; to congeal.

Sākom—brass bracelet ; wristlet.

Sọkor-sakor—to snore : Syn. Hoo-ṭir.

Sāk-sākāo—to drop heavily.

Saktao—to bind tightly.

Sakwa—a big conch trumpet, used in hunting and battles.

Sāl—a year : Syn. Sirmā.

Sālā—a measure of grain ; about 30 to 40 seers in weight : Syn. Kaṭ.

Sālā }
Sārā } —brother-in-law.

Salāh }—advice ; to consult and arrive at an agreement,
Salā } to choose.

Sālāmi—a present given to a landlord for granting a lease.

Sālāngi—tall ; high ; to make full ; to heighten ; to exalt.

Sālgam—turnip.

Salgāo—to kindle ; to lit up (H.).

Salhā—to advise ; to consult ; in agreement with ; advice ; to settle.

Sālis }—to arbitrate.
Sālsi }

Saltant }—absence of any dispute ; relief ; peace.
Salsant }

Sāmā—false ; nothing ; empty ; unimportant ; trivial ; vain ; naked ; uncovered.

Sāmā-ge—empty-handed : Syn. Ipāege.

Sāmā-sāmā—vainly ; in vain ; falsely ; fruitlessly.

Sāmā-te—gratis ; free ; falsely.

Sāmān—equal : Syn. Bārābāri.

Saman—summons (H.).

Sāmāng—to look up with the head raised ; to front.

Sāmāo—to enter (H.).

Sāmbā—iron cap fixed on the end of the pestle (dhenki or sāmāṭ).

Sāmbir—to lie on the back.

Sāmbrāo—to check ; to sustain ; to bring round to proper order.

Samdhi M. }—relationship between parents of a married
Samdhin F. } couple (when addressing each other).

Samdhibheṭ—ceremonial mutual greetings between the bride's guardian and the bridegroom's guardian and the drinking of each other's health.

Sāmpoṛon—to be ready ; ready.

Samjhāo—to explain ; to convince ; to understand.

Sāmāṛo—to manage ; to conduct ably.

Sāmṛom—gold (Sans. Subarṇam).
Sāmṭao—to collect together ; to round up.
Samundar—sea ; ocean (H.).
Sānāng—wish ; desire ; intention ; to wish ; to desire.
Sānāphāna—materials.
Sāndāng—to lie on the side.
Sandes—sweet-meat.
Sānḍi—male of an animal.
Sānḍi sim—a clock.
Sang—companion.
Sāngā—sweet potato.
Sāngā—pith of a plant ; thick round root of a plant : Syn. Dāhā.

Punḍi sāngā—white variety of sweet potato.
Ārā sāngā—red variety of sweet potato.

Sāngā—tattooing.
Sāngāṭ—a wooden pole.
Sāngar—to hunt : Syn. Sendrā.
Sāngen—see Sāgen.
Sāngi-bhāi—companion.
Sāngil—to look upwards by throwing back the head.
Sāngin—distant ; far away ; distance.
Sāng suṛi—a kind of fruit ; a species of snake.
Sāni—to do over again.
Sānj—half a day (H.).
Sānjhia—third (in order of age) (H.).
Sanjog—opportunely ; by chance seldom (H.).

Sanjok / Sanjog }—opportunely ; seldom.

Sanjot / Sanjat }—ceremony of purification by fasting, etc., previous to the day of worship.

Sānju—to keep ; to put in ; to fill in ; tight.
Sānkhā—*lit.* branch ; family branch.

Sanmang—front ; face to face (Sans., Beng. Sammukha) ; in front of ; presence ; to face.

Sanme—close to ; near by.

Sansār—a non-Christian Munda ; a gentile.

Sānsoon—silence.

Sāntāl—a Santal.

Sānti—peace (Sans. Śānti).

Saoār—a rider (H.).

Saodā—goods ; to buy goods.

Sāpāb' }
Sānāpāb' } —reciprocal form of Sab'; struggle ; seizing each other ; hustling.

Sāpārom }
Sāprum } —a kind of tree.

Sāphā—clear.

Sāphāi—to settle a dispute.

Saphar—to go out on tour (H.).

Sāping dāru—a kind of tree.

Sāprum—a kind of tree : see Sāpārom.

Sāpṭāo—to seize with both hands (*cf.* Beng. Sāpṭe dharā).

Sapurad' }
Sāprod' } —to make over.

Sār }
Sā-ār } —arrow ; arrow with iron point (Sans. Sāra).

Sāra—manure (Sans. Sāra).

Sāra gāḍā—manure pit.

Sārā—wife's younger brother.

Sārā jām—materials (Beng. Sarañjām).

Sarāk—the Majhi caste ; a corrupt form of the Jain word Śrāvaka.

Sārā-lijā—cloth given to wife's younger brother at the time of marriage.

Sārām—deer (with horns).

Sāṛāmi—roof.

Sārāṇḍā—an iron rod for cleaning the hooka or hubble bubble.

Sārāngi } —a kind of stringed instrument.
Sārāngā }

Sardār—a chief or headman.

Sarhad—boundary.

Sargujā—a kind of oil seed, *Guisota Abyssinica.*

Sārhul—see Bā'-parab.

Sāre—to leave ; the leavings of one's food (*cf.* Beng. Chhāḍā).

Sāre-ākān—remaining ; remainder ; balance ; savings.

Sāṛi—sound ; to make a sound (H., Beng. Sāḍā.).

Sāṛi—cloth worn by females (H., Beng.).

Sāriāo—to collect together ; to arrange.

Sariphā—the Anona fruit.

Sarjamin—a local enquiry.

Sārjom—sal tree (Sans. Sarjam).

Sarkār—government.

Sarkāri—pertaining to government.

Sarlāhā—rotten ; used contemptuously.

Sarnā—sacred grove in a village, belonging to the village community where the Bongās are supposed to reside and are worshipped and sacrifices are made.

Sarotā—a kind of instrument used to cut the areca nut.

Sarpāo—to curse.

Sār-sār—nails of the fingers ; loosely used for the fingers ; the toe.

Sartāl—to open out an umbrella.

Sārti—true ; truth.

Sārtige—verily ; certainly : Syn. Sāri-ge.

Sāṛu—a kind of edible root.

Sasān—burial ground, where the bones of the dead are buried after cremation (Sans. Śmaśāna).

Sasān diri—burial stone.

Sāsāng—turmeric.

Sāsāng goso—the ceremony of anointment of the body with turmeric, before a marriage (Sans. Gātra-hāridrā).

Sāsāng bād'—a kind of divorce ceremony.

Sastā—cheap.

Sasurāir—father-in-law's house.

Sat }
Sārti }—true ; truth (Sans. Satyam).

Sāṭāo—adjacent; adjoining ; to adjoin ; to put close together.

Sātāo—to persecute ; to give trouble (H.).

Sāṭā sāṭi—close together.

Sā-ā-ting—to endure ; to bear with patience.

Sāthāo—to recover strength after exhaustion ; to rest.

Sātom—the third year from now ; three years ago.

Sāṭpāṭ—quickly.

Sātu—powdered gram.

Sāṭub'—see Singi sāṭub'.

Sāu—a money-lender.

Sāuṛi—a kind of thatching grass.

Sāuṛi-sagun—omen reading by means of grass.

Sawā—one-fourth (Beng.).

Sawāi—interest at 25%.

Sawāl—question ; to question.

Sawānsi—a weaver caste.

Sawād—taste ; tasteful : Syn. Sibil.

Sawāng—strength.

Se ān—adult.

Sebe sebe—to ooze out.

Sekāo—to foment : Syn. Lolo.

Seke seke—chiming sound.

Sekṛā—soon ; quick (Beng. Śighra ; Sans. Śighra)

Sekṛā sekṛā—soon ; quickly.

Seleṭ—a slate.

Sen—to go.

Sen-āyār—to go ahead ; to go before.

Sen-bāṛā—to go about.

Sen-dārom—to go and meet ; to welcome.

Sendrā } —hunting ; to hunt.
Sen derā }

Sengel—fire.

Sengel mār mār—a species of centipede (Beng. Kellui).

Se*n*ṛā—wise ; intelligent ; intelligence ; wisdom.

Sepeṛed'—a youth of twenty (*cf*. H. Samarth).

Ser—to melt ; to dissolve.

Ser—seer ; about 2 lbs.

Seṛān—adolescence ; wisdom ; wise.

Sered'—to tear ; to wear out ; torn ; rags ; to break into pieces.

Sereng—a large flat stone (H. Chaṭān).

Serom—neck : Syn. Hoṭo.

Seser-diri—a stone used to sharpen knives ; a hone : *cf*. Leser-diṛi.

Setā—a dog.

Setā—early morning ; 7 A.M.

Seteng—a natural spring ; to ooze out ; to flow ; flowing ; Syn. Setom.

Seṭer—to arrive ; to reach : Syn. Tebā.

Seṭerni—ambassador.

Sewā—to nurse ; to take care of.

Siāhi—ink.

Sibil—tasteful ; delicious (Sant. Sebel).

Si } —to plough ; to cultivate ; cultivation.
Siu }

Si-chāṭā—to plough for the first time (H. Chirnā).

Siu-ni—one who ploughs.

Sid—to break ; to pluck ; by pulling.

Sidā—previous ; before ; first ; formerly ; ancient times ; preceding, as opposed to Tāyom or Doyā (Sant. Sidāi).

Sidā sim ko rāre—before cock crow (before dawn) ; at the first cock-crowing.

Sidā-ni—the first man.

Sidā re—previously.

Sidā te—from before.

Sidā sidā—the very first.

Sidgir—steep slope.

Sidba—a kind of timber tree.

Sidir bidir—disorderly ; scattered : Syn. Chhitir bitir.

Sidor sodor—to trickle down ; trickling.

Sidub—erect ; to erect ; to keep paddy bundles in an erect position, after harvesting.

Sigid—to tease ; to vex ; to persecute ; to harass.

Sikhāo—to teach ; to tutor (H.).

Siki—a four-anna piece (H.).

Sik*n*ṛi—mosquito : Syn. Bhusri.

Sikṛi—chain.

Siku—louse.

Sikuār—ropes hung at each end of a pole (bāhngi), in which things are carried (H. Sikā).

Silig—a kind of deer.

Silot—slate.

Silping—a screen.

Simānā—boundary (H.).

Sim—fowl.

Engā-sim—hen.

Sanḍi-sim—cock.

Sim-ko-rā—cock-crow ; 4 A. M.

Sim-kusli—fowl shed.

Sim-topoā-ṭāiād—a place where cock-fights take place.

Sināi—rag soaked with the blood of the bridal pair, with which the neck of the pair is touched in token of the mixture of blood between them.

Sindri-Jāng—the backbone.

Sinduri—vermilion.

Sinduri-rākāb'—the ceremony of putting vermilion on the forehead of the bride, during the marriage ceremony.

Singā—to make tattoo marks, with red-hot iron.

Singar—to adorn (H.) (Sans. Śṛngāra).

Sing-bongā—the Supreme God of the Mundas; the Sun God, which, according to them is the visible symbol of the Creator.

Singi—the Sun; hour of the day; day.

Singi-āyub-sā—west; *lit.* the direction of sunset.

Singi-sātub'—all day long: Syn. Singi-buṛā.

Singi-turo-sā
Sing-rākāb-sā } —east; *lit.* where the sun rises.

Sinjo—the bael fruit.

Sipāhi—police; peon (H.).

Sipi—to rub the head.

Siping—to raise up on the palms; to hold a child with both arms.

Sipu—to hiss.

Sir—vein; nerve; muscle of the upper arm.

Sirhi—ladder; stair.

Sirijan—creation; to be born (Sans. Sarjana).

Sirmā—sky; year; heaven.

Sirmā-sing—the Sun God.

Siro soro—to flow through a hole or channel.

Sir panch—headman of a 'Panch.'

Sirtal—to walk unsteadily; to reel.

Sirum—a kind of reed grass; the khas grass.

Sirum-hisir—a necklet of sirum; bead made of sirum.

Si-rurā—to plough for the second time (H. Dobornā).

Sisā—lead (H.).
Sisi—a phial (H.).
Sisirdā—dew.
Siṭhā—insipid ; tasteless ; devoid of substance.
Siṭiā—a small child.
Siṭor—intestines.
Siṭung—hot weather ; heat : Syn. Jeṭe (Sant. Seton).
Siu—to plough ; to cultivate.
Siu-ruṛā—to plough for the second time ; to plough again (H. Dobornā).
Siu-dāṛi-hon—*lit.* a boy fit to plough ; a boy of 12 or 13.
Soāb'—to be full ; to contain ; to take admission.
Soān—to smell.
Soben—all.
Soben sā—everywhere ; on all sides.
Soben tā—all over.
Sobha—beautiful (H.).
Sobo—to pierce ; to poke.
Soboṛo—see Sābṛo.
Sodā—to peck (Sant. Tot).
Sodor bodor—disorderly.
Soe—a sept of the Mundas.
Sohdā—disobedient.
Sohrāi—the ceremony of worshipping the deity presiding over cattle celebrated on the day following the new moon after the Dasai Parab.. The name of the festival is derived from the word "Sohra," *i. e.*, the 16th day after the Dasai full moon. The month of Sohrāi begins from the new-moon day, *i.e.*, the day preceding the Sohrāi festival day, corresponding to September-October.
Sohrāi-durāng—song sung during the Sohrāi festival.
Soiā / Soeā }—rotten (Sant. Seā) ; to rot ; to putrify.

Sojh—straight; to make straight: Syn. Soje.
Sok'-doro—disorderly.
Soke—sad (Sans. Śoka).
Sokhā—a magician; a witchfinder.
Sokṛā—rice field in a channel.
Solom-lotom—mixed up.
Somār—Monday (H.).
So*n*pāo—to entrust; to make over.
Sompoṛo—to get ready.
Sonā—gold: Syn. Sāmrom.
Sonā-didi—the legendary golden vulture.
Sonār—a goldsmith (H.).
Son-chitā—a leopard.
Son-dhāo—to heat an earthen pot in order to sterilise.
Sondro—pus.
Song—to measure; to survey.
Songhā—a narrow path.
Songe—in company of.
Sonjog—by chance: seldom.
Sonong—measurement; survey.
Sonsoroi—a grasshopper.
Sopor—nose (applied to animals).
Sorlo—to pierce.
Sorom—shame; shyness: Syn. Giu.
Soro—a wooden bar placed crosswise to close an entrance (*e. g.*, of a cowshed).
Sonṭh, Soinṭh, Sonṭhā—dry ginger.
Soso—a kind of poisonous fruit, *Semicarpus anacardium* (H. Bheloā).
Soso-bonga—a festival celebrated in the month of August (Ind chāndu).
Soṭā—a stick.

Soṭo—to place in proper order.

Sotopoṭo—dirty : as the hands and face after eating.

Soṭrā—dirty ; impure ; impurity contracted through breach of caste rules.

Su—to thrust the hand inside anything.

Subā—root of a tree ; root ; below

Sud—interest.

Sudhār—to improve ; to correct ; improvement (H.).

Sudhrāo—to improve.

Sui—a needle.

Suj-buj—understanding.

Suk-mur-gonong—bride price.

Suk-muṛ-urij'—cattle given as bride price.

Sukhal—dried : Syn. Roṛ.

Sukri—a pig.

Sukruār—Friday (H.).

Suku—gourd.

Suku—happy ; pleasure ; to be pleased ; happiness ; to enjoy ; to love (H., Beng. Sukh).

Sukul—smoke.

Sukuṛdum—to sit with folded legs.

Sul—any griping pain (H.).

Sulgāo—to kindle.

Sulni }
Suli } —runnings from the nose.

Sum }
Sam } —level.

Sunā—empty ; void ; cypher (H.).

Sundar—beautiful (H.).

Sunḍi—a wine dealer (H.).

Suṇṛ—trunk of an elephant (Sans. Śuṇḍa).

Sunum }
Sunung } —oil.

Sunum-bing—a kind of snake.

Sunum-mui—poisonous biting ant. (H. Lohā chimṭi).

Sunusār—nursing ; service.

Supid—to tie up the hair with a pin or band and dress it (applied to females).

Supṭāo—to intercept.

Supú—upper arm (from the elbow to the shoulder joint).

Suṛā—to shoot forth new leaves.

Surāhi—a kind of earthen water pot (H.).

Surgujā—a kind of oilseed.

Surhi—a kind of paddy-destroying insect.

Surin—a sect of the Mundas.

Surkāo—to tighten.

Surkhi—powdered or ground brick (H.).

Suṛṭāgiti—to lie on the side.

Susār—to nurse (Sans., Śuśrūṣā).

Susāri—one who nurses ; loosely used for a cook.

Susi—to pretend ; to make an excuse.

Susti—lazy (H.).

Susuān—to make a hissing sound.

Susultai—brightness.

Susu-susu—to shiver with cold.

Susun—to dance.

Sutām—thread (Sans. Su'tram).

Sutam-thailā—a purse.

Sutām-tol—the ceremony of putting thread round the waist of a child.

Suti—to recover one's sense ; to be sober.

Sutri—a thin rope of cotton.

T

Tā—to ; forwards ; used as a locative suffix : used as a prefix to personal pronouns, denoting the possessive case, *e.g.*, tāing, tām (my) (your); or as an exhortation, *e.g.*, oṛong tām, bring out.

Tabak tubuk—to make a sound as when swimming (Sant.).

Tābā tubu—walking of little children.

Tabe
Tabe-do } —than ; after that.

Tābedār—servant ; follower (Sant. & H.).

Tabe do—then ; subsequently.

Tābu—our (Sant. Tābo).

Tadbir—to make necessary enquiries (Sant. & H.).

Tadārok—to enquire ; to investigate (Sant. & H.).

Tāeom
Tāiom } —after ; following ; back ; behind (Sant. Tāenom).

Ṭāeād—place ; spot ; space.

Tā-ete—from (some one).

Tāgda—a reminder (H.).

Tāgo—a wild cat : Syn. Bānḍo (Sant. Togot).

Tāgoe—to chew ; to masticate ; to grind the teeth (Sant. Togoeh).

Tagot—strength (H., Sant. Tagoj).

Tāgum tāgum—to eat voraciously (Sant. Tāgum).

Ṭāhrao
Ṭhahrāo } —to settle ; to fix.

Tahsil—to collect (H.).

Tahsildār—a collector (H.).

Tāi—a shallow frying pan.

Tāiār—to make ; to prepare ; to be ready.

Tāikenā—was ; used to ; was in the habit of.

Tāin—to stay ; to remain (Sant. Tāhen).

Tāing—mine.

Tāinokā—let it remain ; let it stay.

Tāiom—See Tāeom.

Tāiom te—afterwards ; behind.

Tājā—fresh (H.).

Tajbij—consideration ; judgment ; opinion ; to consider (H.).

Ṭākā—a rupee (Sant. & H.).

Tākiā—a pillow (H.).

Ṭākrā ṭukru—broken pieces.

Takrār—dispute ; quarrel : Syn. Epeger, Eperāng (Sant. & H.).

Taktā—a plank (H.).

Ṭaku—a piece of wood hung on the neck of cattle so that it may not stray away : Syn. Tuṛki.

Tālā—a lock (H.).

Tālā }
Thāla }—middle ; half (Sant.).

Talab—wages (H.).

Tālānida—midnight.

Tālāo—a tank (H.).

Talbānā—any fee levied for summoning a man (H.).

Tālebar—rich ; big (Sant. & H.).

Tālkā—the palm of the hand and the foot (Sant.).

Talṭul—a sound of anything.

Tām }
Thām }—to beat.

Tāmākhu—tobacco (Sant. & H.).

Tāmāsa—a show (Sant. & H.).

Tamasuk—a bond (Sant. & H.).

Tamba—copper (Sant. & H.).

Tāmbāo }
Thāmbāo }—to halt ; to cause to halt (Sant. Beng. Thāmāna.

Tāmbu—a tent (H.).

Tāmil—to serve a process (H.).

Ṭāmkā ṭākur—miscellaneous articles huddled together (Sant.).

Tāmras—guava (H.).

Ṭām-ṭāmāo—to be in readiness (*e. g.*, for a fight).

Ṭāmuti—untrained ; inexperienced.

Tān-tāikenā—suffixed to intransitive verbs to indicate the present or future imperfect, implying that the action was going on, *e.g.*, Higu tān tāikenāing, I was coming.

Tānā—simple present tense suffix.

Tānā bhānā—to make preparations (Sant.).

Tānā busā—many (Sant. Tānāk busāk).

Ṭānāṛom—rheumatism.

Ṭanḍā—to stand with legs apart.

Tāni—*lit.* Is he, *e.g.*, Ne hoṛo Urāon tāni—this man is an Urâon.

Tankhā—pay ; salary (H.).

Ṭānṛ—upland : Syn. Piṛi.

Tāntāṛā—a wooden platform to keep things.

Ṭāñti—a weaver ; Syn. Penṛāi.

Tānṭi—barren ; past the age of breeding (Sant. Nārchā).

Ṭāprā ṭoprā—small.

Ṭāpu—an island (Sant.).

Tār—wire ; telegraph ; brass armlet.

Tārā—half ; a portion.

Tārā mārā—a few ; a portion ; little (Sant. Tārāntar).

Tāran—shoulder (Sant. Taren).

Taṛbaṛiā—restless ; active (Sant., H.).

Tā-ren—of ; belonging to.

Taṛiā—inferior class of lowland.

Tārikh—date : Syn. Nenḍā (H.).

Tarkāo—to scold.

Tāṛki—a big ear-ring.

Tāṛpat—a kind of ear-ring.

Tārpin sunum—turpentine (Sant.).

Tāṛ sākām—ear-ring of palm leaf.

Tār singi—afternoon ; 3 P. M. (Sant. Tārā Sin).

Tārub′—a kind of tree.

Tārwāir }
Tarwāri } —a sword (H.).

Tāsād′—grass (Sant. Tasak).

Tasbir—picture (H.).

Tāsi—to spread out to dry (Sant. Tāse).

Ṭaskāo—to knock : Syn. Uduṛ.

Taslā—a frying pan made of bell metal (H.).

Ṭāṭ—gunny.

Tātā—grandfather ; father's father (Sant.).

Ṭāṭāi—to benumb with cold.

Tā-te—to (some one); towards ; with.

Ṭāṭi—a screen.

Ṭāṭi—a lamp.

Ṭāṭra—a bamboo mat (H.).

Tāu—sparrow.

Tāwā—a hollow earthen frying pan.

Tāyān—a crocodile.

Tāyār—cucumber (Sant. Tāhir).

Te—to ; from ; by ; with ; sometimes ' in,' *e.g.*, Hoṛote kaji me, Speak in Mundari.

Tebā—to arrive ; to reach ; to be present ; to come up to (Sant. Tebāk).

Tebā tukām—go and reach him (to a certain place).

Te-ko—the family of.

Tej—sharp ; strong (H.).

Tejpāt—a kind of leaf used as spice (H., Beng., Sant.), *Laurus cassia.*

Ṭekad′—to be disturbed.

Ṭekāo—to obstruct ; to stop (Sant., H., Beng. Ṭhekāna).

Ṭeko—to be dried up (said of anything soupy—while being cooked).

Ṭekrāo—to plough for the third time ; to repeat again (Sant. Tekhrāo).

Telā—to spread the palm of the hand to receive ; to hold up ; to bear up.

Telengā-bā—a kind of flower.

Teli—a caste of Hindus ; oilman.

Telsāwār—slightly fair.

Ṭempā—a short stick used for driving cattle, having a knob at one end.

Teng—to weave (Sant.).

Ṭenḍā—hot rice water ; gruel.

Ṭenḍā-ḍang—a contrivance for raising water from a well (Sant. Ṭenādān).

Ṭenḍa-bāiār—rope of the Tenḍā dāng.

Ṭenḍer—to lean upon ; to prop (Sant. Tenḍar).

Ṭenḍrā—a prop.

Tengen—to sacrifice (Sant.).

Tengo'—to carry on the shoulder.

Tenjāng—elder sister's husband (Sant. Tenā).

Tenjāngkoṛā—wife's brother (Sant. Tenāerā).

Ṭeñrā—a measure of grain ; a pailā.

Ṭenṭhā—mischievous ; wicked (Sant., Beng. Ṭheñṭā).

Ṭeoā—a pailā ; a measure of grain.

Ṭeped'—to close an opening (Sant. Tepet').

Ṭepel-hesā—a kind of tree called in Hindi Jitia Pipar ; a form of oath.

Ṭepen-ṭepen—to go along a narrow path.

Terej—three days hence (H. Narsu, Beng. Torsu).

Ṭeṛhā—crooked ; bent ; slanting.

Tersāng—to bask in the sun ; to warm oneself by fire.

Ṭeṭā-dā—pure and clear water.

Tetāng—thirst ; to be thirsty (Sant. Tetān).

Ṭeṭengā—a chameleon.

Ṭethaṛā—disobedient ; obstinate (Sant., H. Thethar).

Ṭewā—a kind of paddy which ripens in May-June.

Ṭhāe—sound of a tree being cut (Sant.).

Thābri—to slap.

Ṭhag—a cheat; a swindler (Sant., H.).

Thaili } —a bag; a purse; a pouch (Sant. and H.),
Thailā }

Ṭhāk-ṭhok—sound (of a hard substance striking another hard substance); to make such a sound.

Thākāo—to be fatigued or tired (Sant. and H.).

Ṭhakbāj—a cheat (Sant., H., Beng.).

Ṭhakbāji } —cheating; swindling (Sant., H., Beng.)
Dāgābāji }

Ṭhakrao—to settle; to decide; to appoint.

Ṭhakrāo—to knock.

Ṭhākur—a barber; a Parha 'officer.'

Thālā-thulu—walking unsteadily, as a child.

Thāl } —to sink as in a swampy ground.
Tāli }

Tham—to beat by a stick.

Thāmāku—tobacco.

Thāmbāo—See Tāmbāo.

Thamkāo—to be stopped.

Thān—a large piece of cloth (H., Beng., Sant.).

Thānā-oṛā—a police station.

Thānādār—an officer in charge of a police station.

Thāni } —a species of wolf.
Tāni }

Ṭhāo—place; spot.

Thāpi—a flat wooden mallet, used by brick masons.

Thāṛā—a brass plate.

Thar-thar—To shiver (with cold or out of fear).

Thāṛi—a smaller brass plate.

Ṭharki } —A wooden bell hung round the neck of a cow.
Therkā }

Ṭhaskāo—to knock.

Ṭhāṭā—fun ; to joke.

Ṭhāṭerā—brassware dealer.

Ṭhāṭrā—a bamboo mat.

Thāui—to draw in ; to pull ; to drag.

Ṭhāui-uṛung—to pull out ; to draw out, *e.g.*, milk.

Ṭhaukā—right, proper, exact, true.

Ṭhaukā-lekā—rightly ; properly.

Ṭhekān }
Ṭhikān } —to find out.

Ṭhekāo—to be steady.

Ṭhelā-ṭhili—to push, as in a crowd.

Ṭhen }
Len } —to get jammed (Sant. Ṭen).

Ṭheo—to stir with a ladle while cooking.

Ṭhepā }
Ṭherchā } —short in stature ; a dwarf.

Ṭhepā—thumb impression.

Ṭhepo—to show the thumb, as a sign of defiance.

Ṭher—to thunder; lightning.

Ṭher-diri—thunderbolt ; flint implements of the stone age are so called as they are believed to have dropped from the sky as thunderbolts.

Ṭhere-ṭhepe—small.

Ṭhesāo—to push, to throng.

Thigā—to trample ; to tread.

Ṭhik—right ; proper ; exact ; good.

Ṭhikā—a contract.

Ṭhikādar—a contractor.

Ṭhikāri—to bask in the sun.

Ṭhikri-putām }
Ṭhirki-putām } —a kind of grey small dove.

Ṭhik-ṭhāk—right.

Ṭhipi—a cork.

Ṭhipsi }
Ṭipsi } —a small bundle of paddy, made of straw.

Ṭho }
Ṭo } —to strike or hit the mark, as an arrow; to knock.

Ṭhokāo—to peck; to strike with something.

Ṭhokar—collision.

Ṭhoko-boko—foolish; ignorant.

Ṭhokrāo—to peck; to rake up old matters.

Thol }
Tol } —to tie; to bind; to imprison.

Tholkānāko—prisoners.

Ṭhonā-ṭhuni—to disagree.

Ṭhoñe }
Ṭoñe } —to break (any hard substance).

Ṭhor—to understand; to remember; to know.

Thorā-thuri—a little.

Ṭhos—to end; to come to an end.

Ṭhoṭhkāo—to peck; to pierce.

Thotnā—mouth.

Thothṛā—a stammerer, to stammer.

Thu—to spit: Syn. Be.

Thukṛāo—to knock against something.

Thuiñ }
Tuiñ } —to shoot with an arrow.

Ti—hand; the forearm; contest; power.

Ti-chompā—back of the palm.

Ti-kāṭā—hands and feet; limbs.

Ti-tālkā—palm of the hand.

Tiāg—to give up.

Tiār }
Teār } —to make; to prepare (Sant.) Syn. Bāi.

Tigā—Same as Thigā.

Ṭi-joṛāo—to join the palms of both hands as a sign of supplication.

Tiju—a small insect ; any insect or worm (Sant. Tejo).
Tiju-hisir—coral bead.
Ṭik ṭorok—a kind of small bird ; the bulbul.
Ṭikā—to vaccinate ; to put a mark on the forehead.
Ṭikāo—to settle ; to decide ; to survive ; to last.
Ṭikait—eldest son of a chief.
Ṭikas }
Ṭikli } —a ticket ; a stamp.
Tiki—to boil paddy before husking ; to boil cloths before washing.
Tikin—midday ; noon.
Tikin-horā—the distance that can be travelled from morning till noon.
Tikin-manḍi—midday meal ; dinner.
Ṭikli—a postage stamp.
Ṭikmin cheñṛe—a kind of bird of the swallow species.
Ṭikurā—a piece of upland surrounded by lowlands.
Til—a kind of oil-seed ; sesamum : Syn. Tilming.
Tilak—coronation ceremony.
Tilāiputām—a species of grey small pigeon.
Tilā-sār—a kind of paddy.
Tilguṭi—a kind of out-door game.
Ṭilhā—a mound : Syn. Bunum.
Tin—tin.
Ting—to kindle fire ; to insert fuel wood in order to kindle fire : Syn. Onḍor.
Tingu }
Tingun } —to stand (Sant. Tengon).
Tingu susun—dance in a standing posture.
Ṭipā—a drop.
Ṭipan—to sew : Syn. Tukui.
Ṭipi-ul }
Ṭipiun } —to float in water ; to rise above the water.
Ṭipsi—See Ṭhipsi.

Tiril—a kind of fruit tree. *Diospyros melanoxylon* (H. Keond, Sant. Terel, Beng. Gab.).

Tiring—to heap upon one another.

Tirmirāo—to feel weak or giddy.

Ṭirsul—one-eyed ; having defect in one eye.

Tirub—to bow the head to worship ; to hang down the head to salute.

Tising—to-day (Sant. Tehen) : Syn. Ising.

Tising gāpā—now-a-days ; *lit.* to-day and to-morrow : Syn. Nimir-ge.

Tisri—cotton cleaner.

Toā—milk ; to give milk ; the female breast.

Toā bāhā
Aṭāl bāhā }—a kind of white flower.

Toākāṭkom—a species of crab.

Tobe—then.

Tobe do—then only.

Tod—to knock the foot against an obstacle ; to stumble (Sant. Torot).

Todārok—to enquire ; to investigate.

Toe
Toñe }—to break ; to fracture.

Ṭokā
Ṭonkā }—to have a hole at the bottom.

Ṭokāo—to challenge ; to question.

Ṭoknā—the ankle.

Ṭoko—a kind of small brinjal : Syn. Bengaṛ.

Tol
Thol }—to tie ; to bind ; to fasten.

Ṭolā—part of a village.

Tolā—a measure of weight.

Tolong—part of the Botoe hanging down in front.

Ṭonā—to cut into lengths (*e.g.*, timber).

Ṭonkā—an aperture ; a hole.

Ṭonki—an elongated bamboo basket.

Tonol—a fastening ; anything to fasten with.

Toñṛang—a jungle.

Ṭonṭo
Ṭonṭomui } —a species of big black ant.

Top—a cannon.

Topā—to bury ; to cover.

Topāni—one who buries.

Topol—reciprocal form of 'tol' ; to bind each other.

Toṛā—a bag ; a purse for holding money.

Toṛāoni
Gonong toṛāoni } —one who settles the bride price.

Toṛe—to insert or bind at the end of the cloth : Syn. Ṭonḍom.

Torkālom—two years hence.

Tormosedsirmā—the year before 'year before last,' *i. e.*, three years ago.

Toṛo—itches.

Toroe—ashes (Sant. toroch).

Tota—naked.

Totā-buṛi—the first woman according to Munda Cosmogony.

Ṭoṭe—to shoot with a gun.

Ṭoṭko—a piece of cloth tied round the neck.

Ṭoṭorā—throat ; windpipe.

Tuar—an orphan ; to become an orphan.

Tubil—marrow.

Ṭuilā—a kind of musical instrument made of hollowed-out gourd fixed on a bamboo rod at one end and a string running through the gourd up to the other end of the rod. The notes are produced by the pressure of the finger tip.

Tud'—to pluck ; to root out ; to pull out.

Tukā—a bird's nest (Sant.).

Ṭuku—mallet for husking paddy (H. Samat).

Tukui—to sew.

Tukui lutur
Lutur tukui } —ear-ring ; to bore the ear.

Tukā—used as a suffix meaning 'to do an act and come away'; quickly ; just.

Tul—to lift ; to raise by holding both ends of a thing.

Tulā—scales of a balance ; to weigh.

Tulāḍanḍi—a balance and scale.

Tulni—one who lifts or carries.

Tulsi—basil plant.

Ṭum—small ; insignificant.

Tumbā—a water-bottle made of hollowed-out gourd.

Ṭunḍu—end ; over ; to end ; to finish ; edge.

Ṭunḍu jāked'—till the last ; as long as life.

Ṭungāo—to break with the fingers, as a sprout or other tender thing.

Ṭunki—a small bamboo basket of a long shape.

Tunur—sting ; rising ; ascent.

Ṭupā—a small bamboo basket.

Ṭupri—a cap or hat (Sant.).

Tupud'—pimples on the face.

Ṭupunḍā—hip.

Ṭupuing
Ṭhupuing } —to shoot each other.

Tur—to rise (*e.g.*, the sun).

Turi—bamboo-basket-makers.

Turiā
Turuiā } —the numeral six (Sant. Turui).

Tuṛ—to sting (Sant. Tor).

Turuk—a Musalman.

Turu-tukā—a squirrel's nest.

Tusā—to break with the fingers.

Tusang—to pick up and collect ; weeding of grass by the hand.

Tusing—to wear ; to put on ; to dress ; to adorn.

Tuskā
Phalnā tuskā } —so and so ; a certain person.

Ṭuṭā—to break.

Ṭuṭi
Ṭoṭe } —a flattened arrow-head ; to shoot with an arrow.

Ṭuṭi—to suffer loss and damage.

Tuṭkā—back of the neck or head.

Ṭuṭki—worn out with use.

Tutkun—cold.

Tuyu—a jackal (Sant. Toyo).

U

Ub'—hair.

Minḍi-ub'—wool.

Ubār—to be saved.

Uber—to clear up after rain (Sant., H.).

Uchāran—to pronounce (Sant., H.).

Uchit—proper ; necessary.

Uchud'—hump of a bull (Sant. Ochot).

Ud'—mushroom (umbrella-shaped) (Sant. Ot).

Ud'—to swallow (Sant. Ut).

Udāl—a prop used to keep carts in position.

Udām—work ; business (used as a suffix to ' kam ').

Udās—to look dejected : Syn. Huṛing jiu (Sant., H.).

Udāsi—curd ; whey (H. Dahi).

Udhār—credit : Syn. Paiñcha (Sant., H.).

Udri-duku—dropsy (Sant. and H. Udri).

Udub'—to show ; to point out ; to explain ; to tell ; to inform ; to accuse (Sant. Uduk').

Udub'-āeār—to prophesy.

Uduṛ—to push ; to throw down.

Uduṛ-oḍong—to expel ; to push out.

Ugur—to hide oneself under a bush or straw ; to insert ; to push into.

Uh'—an exclamation of pain.

Uhirkhārpā—a leather sandal.

Uiyu—to fall off ; to fall down ; to fell (Sant. Ujuk)

Ujaṛ—to dismantle.

Ujur / **Ujur mājur** }—to object ; to file an objection ; objection.

Ukā—the elbow ; to strike with the elbow.

Ukil—a lawyer.

Uktā—to back-bite (Sant. Oktā).

Uku—to conceal ; to hide the upper stomach or pouch of birds where food is stored (Sant. Oko).

Ukuinung—a kind of out-door game, similar to 'hide and seek.'

Ukul-bukul—to be uneasy and anxious.

Ul—to ripen artificially.

Ulā—to vomit : Syn. Hul (Sant.).

Ulār—to heavily load a cart on one side so as to cause the other side to rise up : Syn. Chimṭul.

Ulaṭ-pālaṭ—topsy-turvy ; confusion.

Ulā-uṛung—to vomit ; to throw up : Syn. Ok.

Uli—mango (Sant. Ul).

Ulidā—saliva : Syn. Bé-dā.

Uli-sākhi—a special ceremony connected with marriage. A mango tree is supposed to bear witness to the marriage proposal.

Ulgulan—rebellion ; a state of confusion and anarchy.

Ulphā—useless.

Ulṭā—opposite (Sant. & H.).

Ulṭāo—to turn upside down ; to upset.

Ulṭi—Same as Ulṭā.

Ulṭi-pulṭi—Same as ulaṭ-pālaṭ.

Um′
Umen } —to wash the body; to bathe (Sant. Um).

Umāgā—a form of addressing the mother, used by children.

Umar—age (Sant. & H.).

Umbul—shadow; shade (Sant. Umul).

Umbul āder—ceremony of obsequy of a dead person.

Umi—to become public; to spread, as a rumour.

Umtāo—to become excited; to be mad: Syn. Bālu (Sant. & H.).

Unḍi
Unḍite } —younger uterine brother.

Undub—to be born; birth; to bring forth.

Unḍu—a hole; an opening; to make a hole,

Ungud′—to bend (animate).

Ungud′-susun—dance in a stooping posture—common during the Indchānḍu.

Unṭ—camel (Sant. & H.).

Unum—bath.

Upāe—means; resource (H. & Beng.).

Upal-bāhā—the lotus (Sant.) (Sans. Utpal).

Upās—fast: Syn. Kaṭab (H.).

Upjāo—to grow; the yield of a crop (H.).

Uprā-upri—to strive against one another.

Upun-iā—four.

Upuṭub′—reciprocal form of Uṭub′.

Ur—to dig with a spade; to hoe; leather; hide; skin.

Uṛ—bark of a tree.

Uṛu—to think; to consider; to reason; thought; cares; anxieties.

Ur-usār—to dig and extend, while reclaiming land.

Urāng
Urāon
Orāo′n } —an Oraon.

Urgum—warm.

Uri—bullock; cattle in general.

Uri—tight; to come off, as dried skin (Sant. Ur).

Hāḍā-uri—plough cattle (male).

Siu-uri—plough cattle.

Gunḍi-uri—plough cattle (female).

Uṛiā—a wide-mouthed bamboo basket.

Uriālāng-dā—the bee-hive of the smaller kind of honey bee, of the size of a cow's tongue, hence so called.

Uriālāng-engā—a kind of honey bee of the smaller species.

Urialang-rasi—honey of the uriālāng bee.

Uṛiāo—to collect together and put in proper order.

Uṛi-cheṅṛe—birds indicating good and bad omen.

Uṛid—a kind of pulse; *Phaseolus Mungo.*

Uri-goṅṛā—cattle shed.

Urih'—to peel off.

Uri-hon—a calf.

Uṛij'—a small bird.

Uṛilā—a big bamboo basket.

Uṛu—to mourn; to harp upon something; to remember; to consider; to thrill.

Uru—a beetle (Sant.).

Uṛung }
Oḍeng } —to get out; to bring out.

Nel-uṛung—to search out; to recognise.

Usār—to complete; used as a suffix, also to signify extension and completion.

U-sasān—the 'sasān' where bones are buried, as opposed to 'masāṛṅā,' the place where dead bodies are buried or burned.

Uskāo—to put in paddy or other grains into the mortar while husking.

Uskur }
Uchkāo } —to incite; to stir; to kindle afresh.

Usnā—rice which has been boiled before being husked (Sant. & H.).

Usrāo—to make haste ; to expedite (Sant. Usara).

Usu—to be tired or worn out ; to be weakened ; weak ; thin ; arid.

Usun-usun—a little hot.

Utar—suffix to denote completion of an action ; also used as a suffix to indicate the superlative degree.

Uṭhāo—to raise ; to collect ; to break up camp.

Kaji-uṭhāo—to disregard ; to disobey.

Uṭhāo-pāṭhāo—to take away everything.

Uṭi—knot or joint (of, *e.g.*, a finger, a bamboo pole) (Sant.).

Uṭkāo—to dig out ; to turn over.

Uṭkā paṭkā—to rake up old matters.

Utu—vegetable ; any curry with which rice is eaten ; to stew (Sant. m).

Uṭub'—to charge with horns erect.

Utuñṛu }
Utuṛun }—to uproot ; to dismantle ; to pull down.

W

Wakil—a vakil.

Waronṭ—a warrant of arrest.

ADDENDA

A

Ǻā-sār-kāpi—*lit.* bow, arrow, and axe ; weapons in general.

Abbā—father.

Achād'-uchud'—heaps ; mounds ; uneven.

Achāngā—a kind of shelf.

Achār—to miss one's aim.

Āchār—pickle (H).

Achārā—the coloured border of a cloth (Sans. Añchal).

Ǻchāṛā-chāndu—*lit.* wet-sowing month; the month of Ǻsāṛh. July.

Ǻchu-posoṛā—a variant of Āsu (isu)—posoṛā, meaning to oppress greatly, to misuse one's authority.

Ǻdā—awake ; watchful.

Ǻrā-god—to overlook a fault ; to condone.

Ǻdal—fame.

Ǻdal-bāṛāo—to spend for show.

Ǻdānā—lowly.

Ǻdā-sudā—half (H. Ādhā-sudhā).

Ǻdā-uṛum—to recognise.

Ǻd'-bedā—to mislead.

Ǻd'kā—more (H).

Ǻding-nidā—latter part of the night.

Ǻḍoā-sutām—thread which has not been sized.

Ǻeār-tāeom—both in front and behind.

Ǻgṛā-bāgṛā—promiscuous (H. Ǻgṛam-bāgṛam).

Āgom—to promise a sacrifice in order to obtain a favor.

Ǻhir—a Hindu milk-man.

Ǻind—eel ; a sect of the Mundas.

Āium-āndāj—to guess by hearing.
Āum-āu—to know by tradition.
Āium-gāṇḍe—to hear and misunderstand.
Āium-god'—to hear and treat with contempt.
Āium-hāpe—to hear and remain silent; to hear silently.
Āium-idi—to hear and report.
Āium-jom—to hear attentively.
Āium-muṇḍi—to hear and understand fully.
Aium-nām—to hear by accident.
Ājā-baṛāko—ancestors : Syn. Tātāko.
Ājār—to pour by drops.
Ājgut'—wonderful ; very much ; numerous (H.).
Akaṭ-pakaṭ—all kinds of unnecessary things.
Ākusi—hook ; the hook by means of which cattle are yoked to the plough (*cf.* Sans. Aṅkuśa).
Ākuṭi-bongā—a malevolent spirit which causes tetanus.
Ālā dulā—dear ; beloved.
Ālāe-bālāe—misfortune ; misery ; to be in trouble (H.).
Ālgā—to treat leniently ; to loosen one's hold (H.).
Ālkātrā—coal-tar (H.).
Ālo-kā—ālo joined with the subjunctive "ka" is used to express the negative imperative, *e.g.*, Alo-kāko senā, they shall not go.
Amal-pit—billiousness (H.).
Āmās—new moon (H.).
Āmbā (Āhmbā)—needlessly ; carelessly : Syn. Āthauṛi.
Āmbārob kuṛi—widow : Syn. Rāṇḍiā kuṛi.
Āmburu—a kind of sour fruit (H., Beng. Āmṛā).
Āmboṛo-Sāmboṛo—hastily.
Āmi-dāmi—power ; control.
Amsi—mango dried in the sun (H.).
Anādo—on the other hand ; on the contrary.
Ānā-mānā—all kinds.
Anāpiā—the third one.

Ānār—pomegranate (H.).

Āndṛā—ignorant ; stupid (H. Āndhṛā).

Ān-disum—foreign country.

Ānḍen—jealousy ; to accuse one of conjugal infidelity.

Ānḍu-bānḍu—carelessness.

Ānjar-janjar kāji—an unfounded rumour.

Anṭe—to satiate.

Āngi—stain on a cloth.

Āngop'—to yawn : Syn. chāb'.

Āng-piāṛā-poeoṛo—day light just before sunrise.

Angor—burning coal (H.).

Āngosā—to look with out-stretched neck ; to stare stupidly.

Āngur—grape (H.).

Ānkā-duār—the door of an enclosed courtyard : Syn. Bakṛi-duār.

Ānuṛi—a bolt or peg ; to keep cart wheels from coming out.

Āpābāṛi—to bid against each other ; wager ; bargain ; to shirk and wait for another to do some work (used in a reciprocal sense).

Āpan—one's own (H.).

Āpāpiā—three each.

Āpāṛā—to let out water from a field by making an opening.

Āpārej—to throw water at each other by the hand.

Āpir-med'—a restless and inquisitive eye (used generally with reference to fickle-minded persons).

Āpi-sā—three times.

Apsān-duku—epilepsy (Sans. Apasmāra).

Āṛā—a screen of cloth or leaves to protect from the wind (*cf.* Beng. Āṛ, Āṛāl).

Ārā—a big saw (H.).

Āṛā-ḍil—want of work ; to be negligent.

Āṛāndi-koṛāndi—marriage festivities.

Aṛāng—to take a straight aim ; to go straight.

Aṛāo—to remain quiet and unconcerned, in a defiant manner, preparatory to a fight.

Āṛā red'—gills of fishes ; the depression behind the ear.

Ārāreā—nine each.

Āṛā-sākam-ni—a grown up girl able to recognise the edible herbs.

Āṛā-sāṛā—to be protected by another's power.

Āṛed'—to lower the head while attacking.

Āre-sā—nine times.

Āṛgu-dā—flood.

Ārdās—hope.

Āri—lac in which the insects have died or have flown away : Syn. Phuki.

Āri-āri-giṛi—to feel tired or morose : Syn. Āsid'-giṛi.

Āṛi—ridges of a rice field ; a rice field ; to make a ridge.

Arjom—a kind of ear pendant, usually coloured rolls of leaves or split bamboo.

Ārkāsiā—a sawyer (H.).

Ārmu—the scaly ant-eater ; manis (H. Vajrakīt).

Ārtāng—twilight.

Āṛu—to urinate (used only in a figurative sense, meaning, to suffer from troubles and persecutions).

Āsāndu-dāru—a kind of timber tree (Beng. Mākhāl).

Asid'—to let off an arrow ; to breathe one's last breath ; to die.

Āsid'-giṛi—to be out of breath.

Asul—to pay off any dues.

Asul-hārā—to bring up a boy from childhood to adult age.

Asul-nām—to adopt.

Asul-nām-hon—an adopted child.

Asul-nām-ote—the land set apart for the maintenance of the parents till their death, after a division of the property has taken place. This land is afterwards inherited by the son who supported and nursed the parents in their old age.

Ātāṛni—an incendiary.

Ātar-sunum—perfumed oil.

Ātā-tāben—the name for all preparations of rice which are sold in the market.

Āṭā-māṭā—dense ; thickly grown with trees.

Aṭal bā—jasmine : Syn. Chāulibā.

Āteā—interjection used in addressing persons.

Āṭkār-ichi—to cause to understand ; to punish severely.

Āṭkār kāji—a considered view or opinion.

Āṭkār-uṛung—to understand by introspection.

Āṭkāroleka—perceptible.

Āyo-ge—interjection : O mother.

Āyub-sunum—during the whole day from morning till evening.

B

Bā-āṛgu—to take down by means of a hook ; to decorate with flowers from the top downwards.

Bābā-birhi—a collective name for all kinds of grains (*cf.* Sans. Vrīhi).

Bābā-chāuli—*lit.* pady and rice; meaning, wealth.

Bābā-nājom—a wild variety of rice plant which smothers the cultivated paddy : Syn. Pāsāṛā.

Bā'-belong—a kind of wild fig.

Bā'blā—acacia (H.).

Bā'-buru—*lit.* flower feast and fair ; a collective name for all festivities.

Bā'-chāndu—the season or month of the Bā'-parab (*vide* Bā'-parab) when the Śāl tree blossoms, generally, March-April.

Bā'-gitil—the placenta.

Bāchāṛā—a white intestinal worm.

Bād—to give something into the bargain (Beng. Phāo).

Bad′-bad′-te—with difficulty.

Bādu—antelope.

Bā′-durāng—song sung during the Bā′-parab.

Bāeāng—a thin creeper with edible roots.

Baedā—any castrated animal ; to castrate.

Baemān—dishonest ; ungrateful (H.).

Bāg-dhanu—a kind of tiger trap (H.).

Bāgṛā—a mixture of large varieties of anything.

Bāhingā—a carrying pole : Syn. Mārāṅṛā.

Baisāo—to mortgage (*vide* ante).

Bāiṭre—an interjection of surprise.

Bājuṛiā—a drummer : Syn. Bājāniā, Ru-ru′ni.

Bakain dāru—a kind of timber tree; *Melia Azedarach*, Linn (H.).

Bāksā—corrupt form of the English word 'box.'

Bāki (Bānki)—caterpillar ; a kind of rice plant-killing insect.

Bāku—a many hooked devise to bring out anything which has fallen into a well (H. Jhagar).

Bālāe—difficulty ; hardship ; suffering (H.).

Bālā-merom—goat given by the bridegroom's father or any relation of the bridegroom to the bride's family on the occasion of the Bālā-sākā ceremony.

Bāle—a kind of noose made of thread or hair to catch birds ; to entrap.

Bālisṭār—a corrupt form of the English word " Barrister."

Bālṭi—bucket (H.).

Bāmṛe-mochāo—*lit.* a mouth like that of a Brahmin; abstention from meat ; to be a vegetarian.

Bāmṛe-gosāiño—to adopt the Hindu custom and religion.

Bambar—delirium ; to talk nonsense.

Bāmbāru—a torch.

Bāmbi—a sore that has suppurated after being apparently healed.

Bā'-nā-bātauli—*lit.* neither the Bā'nor the Bātauli; meaning, no festival whatever.

Bānār—trace ; information about a person's whereabouts; a story ; mythology.

Bānchāo—salvation (see Bāchāo).

Bānchāoni—saviour ; protector.

Bāndi (Bāndh)—a poṭom of paddy containing ten kaṭs of paddy.

Bāndāe-bundui—a person having a thick round body.

Bānḍur—to neglect or break off a work or engagement.

Bānitā-kāji—a narration ; a concocted story.

Bānṭhā—stupid ; dull (H., B. Bhonthā).

Bānglā—see under Oṛā.

Bāngāli—pertaining to the Bengalis.

Bānkuṛā—curved.

Bāpāo—to steam something (H. Bhāpnā).

Baṛā—senior paternal uncle ; great grandfather ; great grandson : Syn. Gungu.

Baṛā-honjār—great grandfather-in-law ; father-in-law's elder brother ; husband of mother-in-law's elder sister.

Barāi-ipil—*lit.* blacksmith star. The Capella in the constellation of Auriga is so-called.

Barakāiti—prosperity (H. Barākat).

Baran—*lit.* colour; meaning—kind, variety (H.).

Bāṛāndā-bongā—spirit causing diseases in general.

Bāṛāo—to increase; used as a suffix to other verbs also (H.).

Barchhā—spear (H.).

Bārdulud—same as Bārduṛiād.

Bāṛe (Bāṛi)—the banyan tree.

Bāṛi—feminine of Baṛā ; aunt.

Baṛi-hanar—feminine of Baṛā-honjār.

Barisak—almost certainly (H. Bharsak).

Barkad—inner wood of a tree (*cf.* Borkod).

Barkāo—to slake lime (H. Bharkānā).

Barmā—a gimlet (H.).

Baṛui—to slip off the hand.

Bāsāng—to boil water ; the water in which the rice is to be cooked.

Basut—a receiver ; a vessel (H.).

Bāsi Kusi'ko—food prepared on the previous day.

Bātā—rafters (H.).

Bātoṛo—said of any food forbidden on medical grounds.

Baṭam—corrupt form of the English word 'buttton.'

Bāṭhā—kiln (H.).

Bāṭhi—distillery (H.).

Bāu—to become stale and unfit for consumption.

Bāu-honjār—husband's elder brother (H. Bhāisur).

Baulā—toothless.

Bauṛā—stupid (H.).

Bāu*n*ṛi—instrument for coiling thread from spindles.

Beābi—naughtiness (H. beādbi).

Beānā—a concocted story or version.

Be-bharosā—hopeless (H.).

Begāri—forced labour (H.).

Behos—senseless (H.).

Bejāi—very much ; a fault or offence (H.).

Bejāit—an outcast (H.).

Belāiti—anything foreign (H.).

Bendā—a cross bar : Syn. Ṭāṛā.

Beñdāo—to miss; to lose (H.).

Benṭa—a pole forked at one end, used to bring down fruits (Beng. Ko*n*ṭa).

Bengko—crooked; curved (Beng. Be*n*kā).

Beoṛā—to tie paddy seedlings together ; to tie up the hair.

Bepār—trade (H.).

Bepāri—trader (H.).

Beros—very much.

Beṛā tāyār—sweet melons growing on beṛā land (Beng. Kā*n*kuṛ).

Bet—cane (A., Beng.).

Bhāginā—sister's son (H., Beng.).

Bhajan—a religious song (H.).

Bhārom—a load (H. Bhār).

Bharti—admission (H.).

Bhaṛkāo—sudden fear (H.).

Bhaskāo—to sag (H.).

Bhasṛāo—to loosen and fall off.

Bhāṭu—elder sister's husband (H.).

Bhed—inner meaning; reason (H.).

Bhejā—to hit with a stone or arrow.

Bhengraj—king crow : Syn. Dhe*n*chuā. A sept of the Mundas. A kind of creeper used as a remedy for itching toes.

Bhoko-bhoko—stupidity.

Bhoko-chonḍo—stupid (Beng. Bok-chanḍi).

Bhokoṭo } —blunt : Syn. Ṭupā (H., Beng. Bhothā).
Bokṭo }

Bhomboṛa—a tree, the centre of which has decayed (H. Dhoṛo).

Bhorom-sorom—shyness.

Bhoso-bhoso—soft; flabby ; very lazy.

Bhowrā—spinning top.

Bhowr—a kind of beetle boring holes in wood.

Bhowri—to hawk (H.).

Bhui-nim—a medicinal herb; *Andrographis Paniculata* (H. Kālmegh).

Bhulāo—to forget; to cause to forget; to deceive.

Bibi—a snake, (in the language of children).

Bicha-diri—stones containing ores.

Bichiri—to divide into thin strips.

Bichkāo—dislocation.
Bidasi—banishment.
Biḍḍang-biḍḍang—to limp.
Bibri-debuā—subscription.
Bijuṛu—glans of the penis : Syn. Peso.
Bilaiti—tomato.
Bilaiti-kanṭaṛā—pine-apple.
Bil bilāo—soft; muddy (H.).
Bili—testicles.
Bili-had—to castrate.
Bilkā—to feel pity : Syn. Libui.
Bingāo—to be saturated (*cf.* H. Bhingā—wet).
Bing-hāi—eel.
Biṛāge } —alone; only.
Biṛāng }
Biraspait—Thursday (H.).
Birdisum—forest country : Syn. Tonāng-rāj.
Bitā—a space (H.).
Bo—a form addressing equals.
Bodā-meṛom—he-goat.
Bo-jāmbṛā—In the Hasada country it is synonymous with Bo-kandṛu and means the south, because a dead person is buried with the head (bo) pointing the south, while in the Naguri country it means the north, for the same reason. In the Hasada country, Kāṭā-jāmbṛā or Kāṭā Kandṛu means the north and in the Naguri country it means the south.
Bonjoṛ—to leak out (said of dry grains) : Syn. Bonjong.
Bonḍea—tasteless and insipid.
Bongā buru—collective name for all kinds of spirits.
Bongā daru—cactus (Beng. Manasā plant).
Bongā goe—to kill as a sacrifice.
Bongā sim—sacrificial fowl.

Bor uṛung—to draw out; to reel.

Borā—sack (H.).

Boṛāo—to dry up for want of moisture.

Boroncho do—rather (*cf.* Beng. Varañca).

Boroṛo—slippery.

Boṛ—a thick rope of straw.

Boṛā—blunt; toothless.

Boṛeār—unfit for work ; lazy.

Boṛor—custard apple ; the Anona.

Borsi—a pan in which fire is kept in the winter for warming oneself (H.).

Bosoren—to walk cautiously preparatory to an attack.

Boton—to provide for the future.

Botor—ridge beams on the sides.

Boṭe—to foam at the mouth; drying up of the mouth.

Buāl—to float.

Butukāo—to live in plenty.

Bubusāo—to get mouldy.

Bud—Wednesday (H. Budh).

Budu-hai—a kind of very small fish.

Bukā—the heart.

Bukuru—to express dissatisfaction for getting less.

Bulung-marchi—*lit.* salt and pepper; condiments; to make anything tasteful or acceptable

Bunṭu—the hymen.

Bunum—white ant-hill : Syn. Bhuñru.

Burdulud—flying ant.

Buri-ditā—old age.

Burkā-ipil—the Venus : Syn. Āngo ipil (H. Bhurkā, a corruption of the Sanskrit word Bhṛgu).

Burid—to break by the root : Syn. Tod.

Buruju—a tower (H. Burj).

Busar—to unwind the twists of a rope.

Busu busu—horrid; to get terrified.

Chābu—to touch a liquid with the tip of the fingers.

Chācho—to teach a child to walk.

Chāchu—to lift a heavy object on the palms.

Chādlom—the end or tail of anything.

Chād' lom udub—*lit.* to show one's tail; to deceive.

Chād' lom ugur—*lit.* to draw in the tail between the legs; to back out of anything out of fear.

Chāḍu—to cause to sink.

Chaelā—ornamental; showy; love of pleasure; one adicted to songs and dances. Also pronounced 'Chhaelā.'

Chāe*n*ā—a kind of insect emitting a bad smell, generally found on Karanj trees.

Chāgrā lijā—torn cloth.

Chā*n*i—a pick-pocket.

Chailā—chips of wood (H.).

Chākā—to taste; a wheel.

Chakad'—to cover up a truth; to deceive by lies; false wiles; craftiness.

Chākhūṛā—leaven; condiment (H. Chākhnā).

Chākonḍā—a kind of herb; *Cassia obtusifolia* (Beng. Kālkāsundā).

Chākuli—a net work of rope in a round frame, used to carry earth.

Chākuṛā—a harmaphrodite.

Chāl (Chālāo)—to set lac or silk worm insects on trees for propagation; to lead; to spread a disease by contagion.

Chāl chalan—behaviour (H.).

Chālagi—a rocky place near a water channel.

Chālāk—artful; deceitful (H.).

Chālān—to take away to jail; to take away to depot for recruiting as a coolie.

Chāmṭā—a leather strap to bind the yoke with the plough haft (H.) : Syn. Ur-ṛā nāngli.

Chānā—a variant of Chinā; see Chinā.

Chāndā—the contribution made by a Mundari Khunṭ Kāṭṭi family to the total of quit rent payable for a Mundari Khuṛanṭ Kāṭṭi village, to the superior land-lord.

Chanḍāl—an inferior caste of the Hindus (H.); adultery; rascality.

Chandang—step or stride.

Chandoa—a medal; an amulet worn round the neck.

Chanḍu-chanḍu—every month; monthly : Syn. Chanḍū-mutid.

Chandang-parom—to jump over.

Chankāo—to stew in oil (H. Chhankāo).

Chao*n*-chao*n*—pungent.

Changa—to bifurcate; to keep the legs wide apart.

Chāngirā—a kind of basket (Beng. Chāngāṛi).

Chāpāo—to cover up; to conceal (H. Chhipānā).

Chāpkā—ulceration of the tongue.

Chāpri—a small shed (H. Chhapar).

Chāpuā-ipil—*lit.* the bellows. The two stars at the base of the triangular Kids in the constellation of Auriga are so-called. It represents the bellows of the heavenly Blacksmith, the Capella.

Chapu-tumbid'—to maintain one's parents till their death.

Chapu-tunum—absolute darkness.

Chara—food for animals; bait (H.).

Chaṛa—to desire : Syn. Sanang (*cf.* Beng. Chāṛ).

Chari-kuri—a woman who has been abandoned by her husband.

Cha*n*ṛi—to stretch out or distend.

Chāro—a bastard : Syn. Lambihon.

Chārpā (Chārpād')—the sole of the feet ; to tread.

Chaṭā—to split, *e.g.*, bamboo ; to burst (*cf.* Beng. Chaṭā—split bamboo pieces ; H. Chāṭāi—a mat, generally of split bamboo ; and Mundāri Chaṭkā—a bamboo basket).

Chāṭāo—to lick (H. Chāṭnā ; Beng. Chāṭā).

Chātom-āṛā—a kind of edible herb. (H. Sunsuniā ; Beng. Suṣuni).

Chāṭu-lunḍi—cooking utensils.

Chatur—cunning (H.) ; to deceive.

Chāuli-bā—jasmine.

Ché-ché—bitter, *e.g.*, quinine ; hardship.

Chechā-mochā—bad-tempered.

Chekād'—to stop : Syn. Kesed (*cf.* H. Chheknā).

Chelāng-dāgo—*lit.* fit to carry a chelāng (a small pitcher) ; a girl aged ten : Syn. Bānḍā-dāgo.

Chelā—a disciple (H.).

Chhakam-chhil—to overflow.

Chenḍā—a young male or female of 13 or 14 years of age just before puberty.

Chengnā—a chicken ; a small child (*cf.* Beng. Chengrā—a small child.

Cheṛeā—a shepherd or goat-herd.

Chetān-lātāren—*lit.* to move upwards and downwards ; to waver ; to change sides.

Cheṭe-cheṭe—very hot and unbearable.

Cheṭgar—an expert in repartie.

Cheṭer-ote—exhausted soil.

Cheṭer—to stink of urine.

Chaemān—to disappear ; to vanish, as by magic (H.).

Chāenā-bāenā-hoṛo—a magician ; a juggler.

Chhaur—a village road (H.).

Chhera—diarrhoea of animals (H.).

Chhir—udder (H.).

Chhiti-biti—to scatter (H. Chhitirbitir).

Chichi—a fruit which has just grown and quite tender.
Chigi—to prick with something pointed.
Chihil—to get wide awake; to start, out of fright.
Chij—a thing; goods (H.).
Chik—a Hindu of weaver caste.
Chikin—a female ghost: Syn. Chuṛin.
Chhilan—an outcaste.
Chimad—approximately.
Ching—to neigh.
Chingid—to cause redness of the skin.
Chinhā—sign; mark; mark in token of signature (H.).
Chirgal—careful; cautious; wakeful.
Chiṛiao—to excite anger (H.).
Chiṭā—to accuse falsely.
Chitārā—to ill-treat; ill-tempered (H. Chiṛchiṛāhā).
Chitu—dandruff.
Chiṭu-jo—a fruit the seed of which has not fully matured or grown (*cf.* Beng. Chiṭā—paddy which is not mature).
Chiulā—when; what day: Syn. Chiulang, Oko-bulāng.
Chiur—a kind of flowery shrub which commonly grow on the river banks: Syn. Nāchal-dāru.
Cho—mask, used in dances (H. Chhow).
Chochoboro—to be in a pleasant humour
Chochombā chuchumbi—to seize by the neck and push.
Chod'-molang—hot-tempered; a term of abuse.
Choga—the pointed stalk of any plant left after having been cut (*cf.* Beng. Chokhā—pointed).
Chogo—a nick name for people with slender buttocks.
Choitā—a person with narrow head.
Chokād'—to climb a tall branchless tree.
Choke-lud—the biceps; the swelling of the biceps when struck.
Chokoro—difficult to satisfy; to be dissatisfied.
Chombe—a narrow base of a vessel.

Chomdāng—oblique; slanting.

Chopā—to cut down bushes (H., Chhopnā).

Choṛed'—to pluck or break off the tip or point of anything.

Choṛor—to pour liquid by drops.

Choṭ—force; strength (H. Beng.).

Choṭe—affixed to verbs, with much force and suddenness.

Choṭāo—to cut off or peel off.

Chu—to take a pinch of anything.

Chumbā—any foreign substance which has entered the eyes.

Chuhul—to strive; to desire eagerly; to get wide awake; to be exhilarated.

Chunur—the centre of radiation in the hair on the crown of the head; luck.

Chuṭāo—to be free from anything, *e.g.*, debt, fever, etc.

Chirkud—to turn the ears in the direction of a sound; to be on the alert.

Chuṭi-sarsar—the finger-tip.

D

Dah'—deep pool: Syn. Ikir (Sant. Dāhā; H.).

Dāi—husband's elder brother's wife.

Dākh—vine; grape (Sans. Drākshā).

Dālāo—to lay.

Dānāi-ni— a judge.

Dānāng—a secret; to conceal.

Dārom—against; towards; used as suffix to verbs.

Dayā-sirmā—year of grace (used by the Munda Christians).

Ḍhenchuā—the king-crow.

Dendeod'-ke-te-nel—to look with outstretched neck.

Denej'—entrance; climbing.

Denej'-ṭāiad'—place of entrance.

Ḍerā—to twist anything into a rope.

Dharmi—righteous : ; just.

Ḍhonḍos—the hornbill.

Ḍiḍintān—proud.

Dimi, Diā —lamp ; to light a lamp (H. Diā ; Sans., Beng. dīpa).

Ḍing—to collect ; to accumulate (*e.g.*, water in a pool).

Ḍipā—mound ; a raised ground (H. Ḍhipā).

Dirkā—a lampstand (*cf.* Beng. Derko).

Do—To receive ; to welcome ; to employ in service.

Dos-lāgāu—to accuse.

Doyā-jāng—spine.

Dugo—to release ; to escape ; to fall off.

Ḍuki-chuṛā—wetting the bed in sleep.

Dundur—to deny.

Dungui—short.

Ḍuri—the hip bone.

Duṛui-bāgu—to waste ; to squander away.

Ḍuṭu—stump of a tree.

Du'-u—to release ; to relieve ; to cure.

E

E-eā—eight each.

E-sā—eight times.

En-betar—at that time.

En-re—meanwhile.

En-tā, Entāte, Ente —there ; thither.

Ente-do—but then.

Epen-ḍong Turi, Epelom-Turi —a tall herb the stems of which are used to make flutes.

Epeṛā-epṛi—haggling ; to ask each other to do a thing (H. Odābādi).

Eseng-eseng—to feel oppressed owing to over eating.

Eser—to take possession by displacing something ; to overpower ; to choke ; to possess, *e.g.*, by an evil spirit.

Eskār-eskārte—separately ; by oneself (alone).

Eṭā-eṭā—various.

Eṭā—the second.

Eṭāsā-re—in any place ; somewhere else ; in another direction.

G

Gāded—moss.

Gādel—a crowd ; a multitude ; to assemble together.

Gagar—the quail (H. Titir).

Gai-muchi—the devil's claw ; *Martynia Diandra* Glox, (H. Bāghnakhi).

Gānāmā—noun form of ' gāmā,' rain.

Gaṇḍu-ḍāṭā—the grinding teeth.

Gāpā-tere—three days hence.

Gaṛ—fort (H.).

Gāṛā-ḍhipā—rough ; uneven.

Gāring—aunt ; mother's sister.

Gāring-hānār—mother-in-law's sister.

Gasāo—to insult ; to slight ; to treat lightly.

Gāui—to call by the sign of the hand.

Ge-geleā—ten each.

Gele—a sheaf of corn.

Geneleā—a tenth.

Ger—to gnaw.

Gero*ān*—sparrow.

Geṛ-chon—sister's son.

Gere-Kuṛi-hon—sister's daughter.

Geserāo—to mock ; to ape.
Godar—to scratch with claws.
Goe-ānjed'—to faint.
Goen-goen—to grunt.
Goe-sid'—to die issueless.
Gohoṇḍā-hoṛoko— a crowd of people.
Gojā-kān—dead.
Golāng—tail-pit of animals.
Gonoe—death.
Gore-gote—the armpit.
Guchāng—a smouldering log.
Gu-gum-chu—the coo of doves.
Gulaiñchi—a kind of white sweet-scented flower ; the *Plumeria acutifolia.*
Gum—to sift ; to winnow.
Gur'—to throw down (inanimate).
Guṛlu—a kind of corn ; *Panicnm miliare* (H. Gundli).
Gusiā—master ; headman ; chief officer ; head servant.
Guṭi—small-pox.
Gutu—to pierce.
Guturum—a lair.

H

Hābāng-hābāng—the parts under the armpit.
Hād'-jāpā—to cut near the root.
Hāgā—brother ; friend.
Hāgāko—relations.
Hāikaṭ—to wonder ; to marvel ; to be amazed.
Hākāo—to call ; to cry out (H.).
Hākāo-ni—a crier.
Hāke—axe.
Hākim—judge (H.).
Hāl—moisture ; condition ; recent ; news ; information ; tire of a wheel (H.).

Hālā-jolā—about the time, as opposed to 'Dipli' which means, exact time.

Hāmbud'—to clasp in arms.

Hānāṭing-nām—to inherit.

Hān-betar—at that time.

Handuā-utu—bamboo shoots, used as vegetables: Syn. Kuṛil.

Hāngkari-tānā—to boast (*cf.* Sans. Ahaṁ-kāra).

Hāpāṛomko—shades of ancestors residing in the inner apartment of the house.

Hār-āu—to drive; to bring in.

Hāṛām-hoṛoko—ancestors; forefathers; aged persons.

Hārom—to collect; to make a house-to-house collection of subscriptions.

Hāṛom-ni—a collector of subscriptions or taxes.

Hāṛogā—a wolf: Syn. Teñṛo.

Harop—letter of the alphabet (H. Harap).

Hartā—to serve out a meal.

Hāsu-tān—sick.

Hāṭā—a bamboo winnowing fan.

Hātā—to come out, *e.g.*, of the mouth; anything taken in.

Hātom—mother's brother's wife.

Hātom-hānār—father-in-law's sister.

Herni—one who sows; sower.

Hesā—the *Ficus religiosa.* There are three kinds of Hesā—the Ṭepel-hesā, the Buṭi-hesā, and the Chumān-hesā.

Hiṛiāo—to cause abrasion of the skin, *e.g.*, by dragging over uneven ground (*cf.* Beng. Hiṛhiṛ kare ṭānā).

Hobā-hāsu }—cholera.
Oba-hāsu }

Hon-seṛed'—elder brother's son.

Hoyo-ṭoākānā—rheumatism.

Hunḍi-bā—the jasmine of the jungle.

Huri—a kind of shrub used as medicine : Syn. Sursing ; *Vitex Negundo* Linn. (H. Sinduar ; Beng. Nishindā).
Huṭār—a kind of tree ; *Indigofera arboria* Linn.
Hu'-ukār—to low (of cattles) ; to growl (of leopards).

I

Ichi—a causative suffix to verbs.
Idi—added to other verbs to denote continuity of action.
Ipling—reciprocal form of Iling ; to throng and push each other.
Ising—to burn bricks or lime ; to ferment.
Iril-sā—eight times.
Irirliā—eight each ; eight by eight.

J

Jāi-hon—grand child.
Jal—to lick.
Jambuā-chitri—the black partridge.
Jeṛe-jeṛe—flatulence of the stomach.
Jeṛe māng—a clean shaved head.
Jian—to kill ; to do harm.
Joā-Jāng—jaw bone.
Jonom—noun form of ' jom ' ; eating ; feast.
Jorā / **Jhorā**—the caste of boatmen, who act as ferrymen, in the hilly rivers (*cf*. Jhorā = river or waterfall).
Joṛāo—to count and add.
Julā—a jacket (H. Jhulā).
Jumbuṛi—greedy ; voracious.

K

Kāeom—unexpectedly ; suddenly : Syn. Rokāge.
Kāi*n*-Kātu—a rusty knife.

Kāi*n*ā-kenā—*lit.* 'I will not, did'; it means, 'I refused to do it and said 'no.'

Kāi*n*a-tānā—*lit.* 'I will not, being,' *i.e.*, 'I say I will not do it.'

Kāji-jān-kāji—prophecy.

Kalpāo—to suffer pain.

Kāmi-jom—to earn one's living by work.

Kān kāṭā—the praying mantis : Syn. Sākam-nāuā.

Kānṭā-māri—small-pox of the fatal kind in which the sores are flattened and joined together.

Kaṛad'—spindle.

Kaṛaka-mari—small-pox with thorn-shaped pimples.

Kāṭā jāmbṛā } Kāṭā kānduṛu }—south, in the Naguri country, but north in the Hasada country. The difference in meaning is due to the fact that in the Naguri country, the dead are buried with the feet pointing southwards, while in the Hasada country the dead are buried with the feet pointing northwards. For the same reason, Bo-jāmbṛā or Bo-kānduṛu means north in the Naguri country while it means south in the Hasada country.

Keleng-beleng—to tease ; to molest.

Khā*n*ṛā—a small piece of cloth worn by girls.

Khāsi—a castrated goat (H.).

Kheḍli—a low-caste dancing girl (H.).

Khuṛil—to jump ; to frisk about.

Khurji—property ; riches.

Khu*n*ṭ-rā-nutum—*lit.* names of the Khuñṭ ; genealogy.

Kili—sept. The following are the chief kilis among the Muṇḍās :—Topno, Surin, Purti, Bhengrāj, Bārlā, Guṛiā, Tiṛu, Sāngā, Muṇḍu, Āind, Jojobār, Nāg, Bodra, Soe.

The following are the sub-septs :—

Āldā, Āḍoā soe, Bāṇḍā soe, Bāndo, Bāding, Bāge,

Bābā, Bhuiñā, Barjo, Buṛ, Baṛāiud, Bāl muchu, Boe pāi, Bhāndrā, Bānkirae, Biruā, Bājrā, Boḍo soe, Bārlangā, Champiā, Chuṭu purti, Chhatar, Chiki soe, Champi, Ḍābāngbār, Ḍoḍrāe, Dhanwar, Dhamb, Ḍeṛe sāngā, Enga purti, Ekā, Gomi buru, Gamcha soe, Ghagbari, Hemrom, Heṛenj, Horo, Hansṭuṭi, Hans, Hesā, Hasa, Hobo, Hānsdā, Hani purti, Hāsā purti, Hāi, Hāsārā, Hurum suku, Jomṭuṭi, Jerāi, Jāṛiā, Jatrāmā, Jāng soe. Kongāṛi, Kerkeṭā, Kandulnā, Kulā, Kāndir, Kunkāl, Kolundiā, Bāru Kolundiā, Kāndāe buru, Kouriā, Katiṛu, Kachhuā, Kamal, Lugun, Losāg, Longā lobso, Loguri, Lobgā, Lāng cheñṛe, Mānki, Mundri, Munḍu ichā, Manḍi soe, Oṛeā, Or soe, Pinguā, Pāṛeā, Patra soe. Rāmbṛā manḍi soe, Runḍā, Rurā manḍi soe, Soe hembrom, Samad, Sinduri munḍu, Soe murum, Sinku Sunḍi, Sanḍi Purti, Sarukād purti, Sankurā, Sāl, Tāni, Ṭuṭi, Ṭerom, Thām soe, Tiriā, Tiu, Tulā soe, Til soe, Tuing soe.

Kiring-ni—customer.

Kirsul—irritation and itching of the eyelids causing flow of tears.

Kis—same as Khis.

Kisim-kisim—various (H.).

Kis-tan-ko—enemies.

Koko—curved.

Kolom-parab—the ceremony of the threshing floor, celebrated in the month of Aghan (Nov.-Dec.).

Kosṛān—to parboil rice for making beer.

Koṭhi—a bank ; a business house.

Kouri—to cry aloud ; to make a noise.

Kuā—a well (H.).

Kubi—to bend (Sans. Kubja).

Kuchung—to draw in.

Kudā dāru—black berry tree ; *Eugenia jambolana.*

Kuduṛu—to hop on the ground.

Kuilā—charcoal ; to burn charcoal (H. Koelā).

Kuinṛa-gomke—a cruel master.

Kukulni—sender.

Kul-len }
Kulā-kān } —one sent ; apostle.

Kulup—lock ; to lock up.

Kuṭā—to castrate.

L

Lā'—suffixed to 'om' ; it sometimes means, to give in excess.

Lāgāu—to arrange ; to put on ; to fix.

Lāloā—to stare with open mouth.

Lāmbi-hon—illegitimate child.

Lāmpā—horizontal.

Lāngṛā—lame (H.).

Lāpāng—den.

Lārpā—sole of the feet.

Lasuri—to overpower ; pressure.

Lebe-hoṛo—a gentleman ; a kind-hearted man.

Lengā ti—left hand.

Len-tāiken—pluperfect tense suffix, *e.g.*, Hijulen-tāikenā-ing—I had come (but went away).

Leṛā—curved (said of horns of animals).

Leṛhā—lame ; defective.

Libui—pity ; mercy ; kindness ; to show favour.

Liṭāni—the youngest and last child in a family : Syn. Ṭoā-anjed'ni.

Lolopoto-chābān—to feel unduly proud.

Lom kod' }
Lum lum } —grave and proudly silent.

Loṭākānā—to cleave ; to stick (H. Laṭkāo).

Loṭāo—to return back (H.).

Loug / **Lāig** }—to be on bad terms.

Lougtānko—enemies.

Lu'—to ladle out ; to deal out food.

Lukud' / **Lukuj'** }—to bend ; bent : Syn. Kubā.

Lupu—roasted rice.

Lutur-ārāṛed'—the temple ; the part of the head in front of the ears.

M

Māhā-tere—year before last.

Māin—respect (H.).

Majā—pleasure (H.).

Mā-mā'-ni—the executioner.

Mā-mārāng—greatness ; authority ; force ; vanity ; pride.

Mānāl—beans.

Mānārāng—noun form of ' Mārāng ' ; greatness ; glory.

Manḍli—congregation (H.).

Manḍli-oṛā—synagogue.

Māñṛñā—a dead body (H. Murdā ; Beng. Maṛā).

Māñṛāo—to place on the ground (H.).

Mā-pā-tupuing—*lit.* cutting and shooting each other ; battle ; warfare.

Mārāngen—pride.

Mārāngen-tān-i—one who magnifies himself ; the proud.

Mārāng-dā—a great flood.

Mārāng-gāo—*lit.* the great sore ; leprosy : Syn. Sud'.

Mārāng-mochā—*lit.* to make a big mouth ; to rebuke ; to reproach (*cf.* Beng. Mukh Karā).

Mārāng-o—to exalt ; to praise ; to magnify ; to be great.

Mārāng-uter-ni—the Highest.

Med'kan̄ṛnā—ophthalmia with pus in the eyes.

Meṇḍā—curved and pointed towards the head (said of horns of animals).

Mendnibbor—a large trumpet (H. Rām Singā).

Men-ruaṛ—to reply ; to answer.

Meon-meon—cry of cats.

Mid'-en-jāuā—*lit.* became as one ; combined.

Mimid'
Mimiad'
Momoyod' } —one by one ; one each.

Miṇḍi-gupini—shepherd.

Misā-misā—occasionally ; sometimes.

Misāokā—never at all ; never even once.

Misā-te misā—all at once ; suddenly.

Mod'piṭ—*lit.* one market, *i.e.*, eight days, because markets are generally held once a week.

Momonṛeā—five by five ; five each.

Monṛeāren—the fifth.

Monṛe-sā—five times.

Mon-runuaṛ—repentance.

Muchānṛ—wild ; uncivilised.

Mugāru-ipil—*lit.* hammer star. The Pleiades are so called. It represents the hammer of the Sing Bongā with which he attempted to kill the Pañṛki or the dove which is represented by the Aldebaran of the constellation of the Hyades.

Mukti—Salvation (H.).

Muli—direction ; straight.

Muli-Tikin—just at noon.

Mundurā—a kind of ear ornament.

Murut—image (H.).

Mutu—beam (in the eye).

N

Nāhā—same as Nā.

Nālāek—incompetent (H.).

Nālāni—labourer.

Nāme-hon—heir.

Nāng—variant of Nāgen.

Nāñṛe-renko }
Nāpāṛe-renko } —neighbours ; those living close by.

Nāpāṛe—near about ; neighbouring.

Nātāing—husband's elder brother's wife.

Nāo—exclamation used by ploughmen directing the cattle to move to the left.

Nātin—variant of Nāgen.

Ne-lekā-ge—in this way ; verily.

Nel-rikā—to cause to be seen ; to be visible.

Ne-nel-med'-te—in the sight of on lookers ; openly publicly.

Nenḍe—hither.

Ni-ete—from him.

Nimiāng—so much so.

Nimir-ge—now ; now-a-days ; for the present.

Nirmunḍ—*lit.* without a head ; completely.

Nitir—to spread a good report, as opposed to 'Umi'—to spread a bad report.

Nutum-ten—called by name.

Nutum-teni—the one called so and so.

O

Obā—cholera.

Obor-cheñṛe—a bird of the cuckoo species of grey colour.

Oiong—to boil any root or vegetable in water.

Okā-uki-horā—a steep path.

Okil—pleader (H. Wakil).

Oko-āte—by what ; whence.

Okotāte—whence.

Olbāl—the art of writing.

Ol-rikā—to cause to be written.

Omo'ni—the giver.

Onom } —gift.
Enem }

Opom—reciprocal form of 'Om' ; to give each other ; to exchange, *e.g.*, a wedding ring.

P

Pabitra-Ātmā—the Holy Ghost.

Pachh-tāp } —repentance (H.).
Paschanttāp }

Pānchāl—cunning ; crafty (*cf.* Beng. Peñchal).

Panṛki-ipil—*lit.* the dove star. The Aldebaran is so called.

Pāri—turn ; time ; period ; age ; days (H., *cf.* Sans. Paryaya).

Pārkom—Kumṛu ipil—*lit.* bedstead thief star. The stars epsilon, zetā and eta of the Ursa majoris are so called.

Pāsri-ipil—the star at the vertex of the triangular Kids in the constellation of Auriga, is so called. It represents the charcoal fire of the heavenly blacksmith—the Capella, while the two stars at the base of the triangle are called 'chapua ipil,' which represents the bellows of the blacksmith.

Pāṭe—to give up ; to wrap up anything round the waist,

Pātki } —a measure of grain : Syn. Teoā.
Pāti }

Pere—to fill.

Peṛe-jān—able ; mighty.

Peso—glans of the penis ; to uncover the glans.

Phāsāhā—corrupt form of the English word 'Passover.'

Phāsiār—hypocrite.

Pheroāi—to trade (*cf*. H. Pheri).

Phuli—strong distilled liquor.

Pilet—corrupt form of the English word 'plate.'

Piṛi-paṛte—privy : Syn. Piṛi-sā-te or Dā-sā-te (*cf*. H. Pāni-bāṭe).

Poṛo—blind ; blindness.

Poṭom-oṛā—barn.

Puchid'—to reveal one's mind.

Punḍi-diri—white stone ; marble.

Punuchid'—revelation.

Purā-sā—many times ; very often.

Purā-te—chiefly.

—

R

Ramal—variant of 'Rabal.'

Rāngāini-jānum—a thorny plant with yellow flowers : Syn. Lārpā ṭoko (Beng. Siālkā*n*ṭā) ; *Argemone mexi cana.*

Reāṛ—see Rāṛe.

Ribribi—an annual grass with thorns which sticks to clothes.

Ribu—a man with a shrivelled-up buttock.

Riḍid'—gnashing of teeth.

Rikā-lāgāting-teā—what is required to be done ; duty.

Rimbil-saṛi—thunder-clap.

Rinṭi—to deny stubbornly.

Ri*n*ṛi-jom—to borrow.

Ri*n*ṛi-om—to lend.

Ri*n*ṛi-jomā kād'-i—debtor.

Ronod'-kāji—promise ; covenant.

Ros—force (H.).

Runju—scab of a sore.

Rungkā—pointing straightforward (said of horns of animals).

Rup—feature (H.).

Ruṛung—the Palas creeper ; *Bauhinia Vahlii.*

S

Sāi*n*tre—perchance (H. Sāi*n*t).

Sāju—to put in ; to fill in ; to keep.

Sākam-nauā—the praying mantis.

Sākam-tukni-chenṛe—the tailor bird : Syn. Tininini.

Sākṛāo—to encompass ; to put in a difficult position.

Sālāngi-uter—the highest.

Sālom—muscles on the sides of the spine.

Sāmpāṛāo
Sāpṛāo } —to adorn : to be dressed and ready.

Sānḍāsom
Sā*n*ṛāsom } —a big tong (H. Sanṛsi).

Sarāsari—a rent suit ; to sue for rent (H.).

Sārdi—harvest time ; the Hindi months of Kartik and Aghan (October-November) ; cold season (*cf.* H. Sardi=cold, and Sārdiā=pertaining to the season Sarat).

Sāṛgiā—wife's sister's husband.

Sāri
Sārti } —true ; truth.

Sāri—to know.

Sāriṛotān—to overflow.

Sārsanḍi—scales of fishes and snakes.

Sārsing-duku—itching toes (Beng. Pā*n*kui).

Sātār—to shut up ; to barricade (H. Ārgāṛ).

Senger—to throw back the head in order to look up.

Senken-hoṛoko—the men who have gone. 'Ken' is the past participle suffix which converts the verb into an adjective.

Senojān—*lit.* gone ; last, *e.g.*, senojān chāṇḍu=last month ; senojān sirmā=last year.

Sesen—to continue to walk ; to be in the habit of walking ; to follow. Reduplication of verbs is used to denote continuation, as well as to denote a future participle, *e.g.*, se-sen hoṛoko—the men who will go.

Setā-idāng—very early.

Sikid' sikid'—to sob, owing to fulness of heart.

Sikuār bājā—the lower net-like part of a carrier's rope.

Simko-āuriko-rāre—before cock-crow.

Sinibil—sweetness ; good taste.

Singi-ḍubui—sunset ; evening.

Singi-hā*n*ḍe-jānā—the sun has slanted towards the west, *i.e.*, it is 3 P.M.

Singi-hāsur-imtā—at sunset.

Singi-mānḍi—noon-day meal.

Singi-turtānre
Singi-turo-re } —at sunrise.
Singi-oltānre

Siṛibiṛi-kāji—filthy language.

Siril-siril—to feel a vomiting tendency (Sant. Serer-serer).

Sirip—only : Syn. Eskār (H. Sirf).

Siris dāru—a kind of tuber tree.

Siristādār—a court official (H.).

Sirjāo—to create ; to be born (H. Srijan).

Sirmā-phoud—heavenly host ; angels.

Sirmā-ren-dāsiko—*lit.* servants of the Heaven ; angels.

Sirmā-ruāṛ-ruāṛ—every year ; annually.

Sirni—gift ; offering (H.).

Sī-soe—to be calm ; silent.

Sitirkad'—a prickly herb, the ashes of which are used in the preparation of rice bread (H. Chirchiṭi ; Sans. Apāmārga), *Achyranthus aspera.*

Soe—to light a lamp.

Sonpat—hysteria.

Stuti—prayer.

Sud'—leprosy.

Sūḍ'—pit ; well ; a deep pool of water.

Suid'—to mix ; to make a paste by mixing with water.

Sugaṛ—goodly.

Sukuār—lasciviousness.

Suku-kāji—gospel.

Sul—dysentery.

Arāsul—dysentery with bleody mucous.

Punḍisul—simple dysentery in which blood is absent.

Suṛ sing—a medicinal plant (H. Sinduar; Beng. Nishindā *Vitex Negundo.*

Suṛun—shelter ; cover.

Susuntān-ipil—twinkling star.

Suṭi—snail (H. Ghunghi).

T

Tāben—parboiled paddy beaten quite flat (H. Chiuṛā).

Tāben-bā—Chiretta ; *Swertia affinis.*

Tāben—your (dual).

Tāber—to bend forward.

Tā-e—his or her.

Tā-re—with ; near about ; around.

Tāking—their (dual).

Tāko—their (more than two).

Tākui—to spin (*cf.* H. Takuā—a spindle)

Tālā-sārsār—the middle finger.

Tālāng—your and my.

Tāle—their and my.

Tāling—his and my.

Tālsā—roasted rice.

Tām—your.

Tān—present participle suffix, meaning 'to be.'

Tāni—a wild dog.

Tāngi—to wait for somebody's arrival.

Ṭāṛā—cross-bar to fasten a door.

Tārā-molong-hāsu—headache on one side of the head.

Tārā—to lean on one side.

Tāṛom—to cross over from one side to another ; to desert.

Tārwā—palm of the foot.

Tāui—see Thāui.

Te—, Chi— } —used as a suffix to form participle of the definite imperfect—jān, len, ken, etc. ; Seṭer jān-chi ḳāji-kedāe—having arrived, he said.

Telāo—to be received ; to be accepted : to be held in esteem.

Tenelā—receiving on the palm.

Teñrño—wolf.

Ṭeo—see Ṭheo.

Ṭeṛeng—the front portion of the tibia of the leg.

Ṭhāhrāo—to settle ; to decide ; to appoint.(H.)

Thok—crowd ; multitude (*cf.* H. Thok—a cluster).

Ti-kāṭu—fingers of the hand.

Ṭid'lāng—to erect the tail through fear or any other cause.

Tilming—sesame (H. Til).

Tinge-sān—fuel wood.

Tingu-hopor—to stand near by.

Todā—the act of stumbling ; sin ; offence.

Ṭo'-o—to fall into one's hand or power.

Ṭonāng-rāj—forest country.

Ṭonāng-utu-āṛā—a kind of creeper : Syn. Bhais-jamburu-nāṛra.

Ṭoṇḍom—to bind at the end of a cloth : Syn. Toṛe.

Topā-gāṛā—grave.

Topā-ṭāiād'—burial ground.

Torsā }
Torā } —immediately ; quickly ; only.

Torod'—a big lizard (H. Goe-ṭeṭengā ; Beng. Go-shāp).

Ṭoṭā—to break ; to break by plucking (*cf.* H. Tuṭnā—to break).

Ṭumpu—blunt.

Tuṛiām—to pluck.

Tuṛu—squirrel.

Tuyu-sāgā—a kind of prickly grass, the ends of which stick into clothes.

U

Uchuṛu-chumbuṛu—eagerness ; impatience.

Udublāi-hoṛo—a defamer ; calumniator.

Udublāi-kāji—calumny ; defamation.

Uiyun—to put on cloth or garment.

Ukuṛi—to pour out : Syn. Ā*n*ṛ*n*e.

Unḍite }
Unḍite-te } —younger brother.

Undub'—to be born ; to bring forth ; birth.

Uri-āder-dipli—*lit.* the time of cattle entering cowshed ; dusk.

Uri-mānḍā—a general name for birds of the sparrow species ; the finch lark.

Urub'—to burn.

Urui—see Rui.

Uṭungi—plllow : Syn. Koṭ*n*oṛ*n*e or Kuṛu*n*ṛi.

ERRATA

Page	*Line*	*For*	*Read*
8	22	Āpe—more than two	Āpe—you (more than two),
,,	23	Āpeā—you (more than two)	Āpeā—your (more than two)
20	13	be with child	to be with child
,,	28	Bādleṭā	Kadleṭā
26	32	Chādrā	Chāṛrā
36	16	Dānom	Ḍānom
38	29	Darpoeñ	Ḍarpoeñ
40	14	Omtukā	Omrikā
,,	32	Dhembā	Ḍhembā
47	21	Ḍidi	Didi
50	3	Do	Dolā
52	10	Ḍudugar	Dudugar
54	10	B. Odege	Bodege
65	11	Halwāi	Hālwāi
66	20	Hāu	Hār
69	3	that; side	that side
,,	25	his cough	hiccough
70	8	a safoetida	assafoetida
,,	24	time	tense
72	7	Munḍāsi	Munḍāri
76	28	Priul	Iriul
80	5	Jānās-jānāo	Jānāo-jānāo
,,	22	sung at	sung in
83	5	flash	flesh
,,	21	Jin-jatan	Jiu-jatan
84	8	eating for the purpose of eating	eating; for the purpose of eating
,,	32	Joā	Joār
98	3	beef	leaf
,,	21	thief star. The Ursa major	thief driver star. The Alcor of the Ursamajor
99	1	Cheest	Chest
,,	20	to go between	a go between
102	3	tell	tall
110	9	Lukum	Luṭkum
111	9	new years	next year
,,	26	Mahimāu	Mahimān
113	5	a fair to set one's foot	a fair; to set one's foot
115	28	gum; boil	gumboil
123	30	Nā-jānā	Jā'—nā
124	26	Nāg-hing	Nāg-bing
125	15	Nahsr	Nahar
129	32	Nel-okā	Nelo'kā
131	9	Nidariā	Niḍariā
133	18	Nirsusun—Syn. Senojān chanḍu	Nirjān chanḍu—Syn. Senojān chanḍu
139	1	Orā dur	Oṛā-duār

140	6	Tagah jamin	Jagah-jamin
145	1	Parwān	Parwānā
146	2	Patiās	Patiār
,,	3	Pātiā	Pāṭiā
147	6	Jom-mu-perā	Jom-nu-peṛā
152	1	uncleaned	unclean
153	3	Kul-beui	Kul-leni
155	1	Keṛā-ān	Keṛā-āu
,,	7-9	Rābāng—to be light etc,	Rābāl—to be light etc.
158	13	even these	even then
,,	31	used as in suffix	used as a suffix
159	18	Rere-in	Rere-ni
164	16	Sādān-horo	Sādān-hoṛo
165	28	signature to sight	signature ; to sign
168	9	clock	cock
,,	25	Sānjhiā	Sānjhilā
,,	27	by chance seldom	by chance ; seldom
169	22	Sans. Sāra	Sans Śara
,,	24	Sāra	Sārā
170	10	Chhāḍā	Chhārā
,,	12	sāḍā	sāṛā
172	34	to pluck ; by pulling	to pluck by pulling
173	24	silig	silib
177	12	suk mur	suk-nur
178	11	sect	sept
179	6	than	then
180	11	Tuṛki	Ṭhaṛki
181	6	Higu	Hiju
,,	18	Tānti	Tānti
,,	19	Tānṭi	Ṭānṭi
184	13	Thakrāo	Ṭhāhrāo
186	16	Ṭhorā thuri	Ṭhoṛā-thuṛi
,,	25	contest	control
189	26	Tuar	Ṭuar
191	20	hull	bull
192	14	to hide the upper	to hide ; the upper
194	21	Oḍeng	Oḍong
196	27	Sect	Sept
197	2	Aum	Aium
200	21	pady	paddy
202	32	Bāṛi	Baṛi
205	4	Bihri debuā	Bihri-ḍebuā
,,	23	pointing the south	pointing to the south
206	17	Butukāo	Bubukā
,,	28	Buri dita	Buri dilā
207	9	adicted	addicted
208	2	haft	shaft
210	25	Chod'-molang	chod'-molong
213	30	Geṛchon	Geṛe-hon
225	9	Sākam-tukni	Sākam-tukui
226	27	tuber tree	timber tree
229	29	Kuṛuñṛi	Kuṭuñṛi